W9-BYN-182

DNA
on Trial

Glen Cove Public Library
4 Glen Cove Avenue
Glen Cove, New York 11542-2885

Look for these and other books in the Lucent Overview series:

Abortion
Acid Rain
Adoption
Advertising
Alcoholism
Animal Rights
Artificial Organs
The Beginning of Writing
The Brain
Cancer
Censorship
Child Abuse
Children's Rights
Cities
The Collapse of the Soviet Union
Cults
Dealing with Death
Death Penalty
Democracy
Drug Abuse
Drugs and Sports
Drug Trafficking
Eating Disorders
Elections
Endangered Species
The End of Apartheid in South Africa
Energy Alternatives
Espionage
Ethnic Violence
Euthanasia
Extraterrestrial Life
Family Violence
Gangs
Garbage
Gay Rights
Genetic Engineering
Global Resources
The Greenhouse Effect
Gun Control
Hazardous Waste
The Holocaust
Homeless Children

Human Rights
Illegal Immigration
Illiteracy
Immigration
Juvenile Crime
Memory
Mental Illness
Militias
Money
Multicultural America
Ocean Pollution
Oil Spills
The Olympic Games
Organ Transplants
Ozone
The Palestinian-Israeli Accord
Pesticides
Police Brutality
Population
Poverty
Prisons
Rain Forests
The Rebuilding of Bosnia
Recycling
The Reunification of Germany
Schools
Smoking
Space Exploration
Special Effects in the Movies
Sports in America
Suicide
Terrorism
The UFO Challenge
The United Nations
The U.S. Congress
The U.S. Presidency
Vanishing Wetlands
Vietnam
Violence in the Media
Women's Rights
World Hunger
Zoos

DNA on Trial

by Tina Kafka

LUCENT BOOKS

An imprint of Thomson Gale, a part of The Thomson Corporation

THOMSON

GALE

Detroit • New York • San Francisco • San Diego • New Haven, Conn. • Waterville, Maine • London • Munich

Acknowledgments

Many people deserve thanks for their encouragement and support during this process: Ethan Bier, the geneticist who helped me unravel the mysteries of DNA; Oliver Ryder, who put me in touch with wildlife DNA experts; my editor, Marla Felkins Ryan; my son Ben, who is an expert researcher and patiently guided me through the endnotes process on Microsoft Word; my daughter Abigail, who applauded my progress and offered gentle suggestions about wording; my son Simon, who helped me focus; and my husband Zoltan, who is always there for me in every way and offers constant support.

Dedication

This book is dedicated to my family: my parents who have always encouraged me, my husband who believes in me and keeps me calm, and my three beautiful children with whom I proudly share my DNA.

© 2005 Thomson Gale, a part of The Thomson Corporation.

Thomson and Star Logo are trademarks and Gale and Lucent Books are registered trademarks used herein under license.

For more information, contact
Lucent Books
27500 Drake Rd.
Farmington Hills, MI 48331-3535
Or you can visit our Internet site at http://www.gale.com

ALL RIGHTS RESERVED.
No part of this work covered by the copyright hereon may be reproduced or used in any form or by any means—graphic, electronic, or mechanical, including photocopying, recording, taping, Web distribution, or information storage retrieval systems—without the written permission of the publisher.

Every effort has been made to trace the owners of copyrighted material.

LIBRARY OF CONGRESS CATALOGING-IN-PUBLICATION DATA

Kafka, Tina, 1950–
    DNA on trial / by Tina Kafka.
        p. cm. — (Overview series)
    Includes bibliographical references and index.
    ISBN 1-59018-337-1 (hardcover : alk. paper)
        1. Forensic genetics—Juvenile literature. 2. DNA fingerprinting—Juvenile literature.
I. Title. II. Series.
    RA1057.5.K34 2004
    614'.1—dc22

                                                                          2004010677

Printed in the United States of America

3 1571 00226 9564

Contents

Introduction

DEOXYRIBONUCLEIC ACID, OR DNA, exploded onto the criminal justice scene a mere twenty years ago. Its arrival was stunning. Right away it seemed that the police had a tool that could cull order out of the chaos of crime scenes and quickly separate the guilty from the innocent.

Understanding the structure of DNA is one of the most remarkable scientific advances of the past fifty years. The applications that will result from this breakthrough have only begun to be known. The tiny DNA molecule spells out the fate of each cell in every living organism. Whether that cell becomes part of an ant or an anteater, a daisy or a rose, or even a liver or a heart depends on the unique arrangements of the rungs of this molecule that is shaped like a spiraling, twisted ladder. And even as scientists continue to struggle to understand exactly how it works and how to use this information, DNA has become firmly planted as a tool of criminal justice. In a mere twenty years, DNA has become indispensable for solving crimes in which blood, skin, hair, saliva, and other body tissue provide telltale genetic fingerprints.

It was DNA that helped solve the mystery of what happened to seven-year-old Danielle van Dam, who disappeared from her bedroom in San Diego one February night in 2002. Police soon became suspicious of a neighbor, David Westerfield, who explained his absence from home the weekend of Danielle's disappearance by telling police he had taken a meandering, 560-mile road trip in his motor home. But a tiny blood spot on his jacket and another on the floor of his RV filled in a part of his story that he left out when he talked to the police. DNA confirmed that the chances that the blood spot on the jacket, which matched the blood stain on the floor, did not belong to Danielle was 1 in 170 quadrillion. A number like that is astounding, considering that the entire population of the earth is only about 6 billion. To understand the magnitude of that number, imagine placing a single postage stamp somewhere on the vast Texas landscape. The chance of blindly putting a finger down on that exact spot is about 1 in a quadrillion. DNA also identified Danielle's long, blond hair in Westerfield's bed, the sink of his RV, and his laundry. Westerfield's adamant denials were no match against the probabilities

For more than twenty years, DNA evidence has been admitted in criminal cases, including the infamous O.J. Simpson murder trial (pictured).

Irrefutable DNA evidence collected from David Westerfield's clothing and RV helped convict him of the murder of Danielle van Dam in 2002.

that he had murdered the little girl. It was enough to convince a jury not only to convict him of her murder, but to recommend that he be given the death penalty.

DNA has not only given prosecutors a new and highly accurate means of identification, it has also raised the standards for everyone who is involved in the criminal justice system. Police investigators, lab technicians, criminalists, forensic scientists, attorneys, and judges—all those involved in the search for justice—are being held to ever higher standards because this minute molecule is the new lie detector and reality checker. DNA can uncover the truth when an old crime has gone unsolved for many years. Over time, bodies age and memories fade, but DNA never changes. A tiny baby boy and the old man he becomes have the same genetic fingerprint.

Even as scientists untwist this molecule and understand its functions, mysteries remain. DNA can reveal who was at the scene of a crime and who was not, but it cannot tell why the crime occurred. DNA does not judge. It does not decide whether a motive is justified or what punishment should result from a crime. Those decisions are left to human beings. Human beings bear the responsibility to weigh all the evidence and make decisions that are rooted in justice.

1

A Powerful New Crime-Solving Tool

WHEN A CRIME is committed, something is always left at the scene of the crime, and something else is always carried away by the criminal. Those things are evidence. Fifty years ago, two scientists made a discovery that would give forensic specialists a powerful new tool to analyze that evidence. James Watson and Francis Crick, who worked together at Cambridge University in London, discovered the structure of the deoxyribonucleic (DNA) molecule. They did not realize it at the time, but their discovery that DNA is a double helix curled up inside the cell's nucleus would change the course of criminal investigation. Evidence from crimes would no longer be limited to things that could be seen, touched, or heard. DNA evidence, invisible to the naked eye, had the power to identify who had or had not been present at the scene of a crime. Barry Scheck and Peter Neufeld, defense attorneys best known for their work on behalf of the wrongly convicted, explain in the book *Actual Innocence* why DNA fingerprinting is so important to the criminal justice system: "DNA testing is to justice what the telescope is for the stars: not a lesson in biochemistry, not a display of the wonders of magnifying optical glass, but a way to see things as they really are."[1] DNA evidence changed criminal science forever.

The first criminal case involving DNA evidence was solved in England only twenty years ago. The exciting new technology almost immediatedly leaped to the shores of the United States. But despite its promise and some early successes, the introduction of DNA testing to the United States was highly controversial. There were problems to overcome before this new technology could be fully embraced in this country.

DNA makes its grand entrance

The first criminal case involving DNA began with the murder of a young girl in the English countryside. Lynda

Scientists James Watson (right) and Francis Crick discovered the double-helix structure of DNA in the 1950s.

Rungs on a Ladder: The Structure of DNA

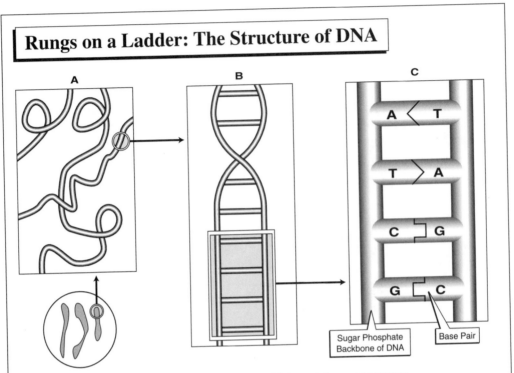

A **B** **C**

A < T

T > A

C G

G C

Sugar Phosphate Backbone of DNA

Base Pair

A. A chromosome is a chainlike strand of DNA, which contains many genes.

B. When the chromosome is greatly magnified under a microscope, it looks like a long ladder that is twisted into a double helix. The twisting allows these amazingly long strands to fit inside a single tiny cell.

C. The sides of the DNA ladder are made of sugar and phosphate molecules. Between the two sides are rungs made up of the four base pairs—AT, TA, CG, and GC. The letters stand for the four bases that make up the pairs: adenine, guanine, cytosine, and thymine. A single strand of DNA may contain billions of rungs. The different arrangements of these four base pairs are codes that call for different combinations of amino acids. Amino acids combine to make up proteins, which, in turn, direct the endless variety of features that make up every living thing. Each sequence of base pairs that contains the instructions for making a single protein is called a gene.

Mann, a fifteen-year-old babysitter from Narborough, a small village in England, never made it home one cold night in late November 1983. Her mother was frantic. In the dawn light of the following morning, her lifeless body was discovered by a hospital worker on the Black Pad, the name given to a footpath that divides the local psychiatric hospital from a cemetery. She had been raped and strangled. Although semen stains were recovered from her body, her murder remained unsolved.

Then, three years later on a Saturday in August 1986, another young girl was murdered in the same small English village. Dawn Ashworth, also fifteen, was out visiting friends one evening and never returned home. The afternoon headline in the local newspaper reported that Narborough police with tracking dogs were searching for the missing girl in the same area in which Lynda Mann had been found murdered three years earlier.

Two days later, Dawn's body was discovered in a field near Ten Pound Lane, another footpath. Again, the cause of death was strangulation, and once again, the young girl had been raped. It was not long before a seventeen-year-old hospital worker named Richard Buckland was under suspicion. Buckland even mentioned to one officer that he had walked with Dawn on the night she was murdered. That was enough information for the police to arrive at Buckland's home at five o'clock in the morning on August 8, 1986, and arrest him for murder. But, though Buckland admitted having spent time with Dawn, he denied at first that he had murdered her.

The police questioned Buckland for hours, and finally, he confessed. But, though authorities were convinced that the two murders had been committed by the same man, Buckland refused to confess to the first murder.

A new type of fingerprint

The police needed more information to prove that Buckland was guilty of the murders of both young girls. They were hoping that Buckland's guilt in both cases would be confirmed by a new process that was being developed in a laboratory not far from the scene of the grisly crimes. Dr. Alec Jeffreys, a geneticist, was working in his laboratory at Leicester University on a technique he called "genetic fingerprinting." Jeffreys was using the recent discovery that cells found in blood, skin, saliva, and semen—cells often left at crime scenes—contain DNA. Since no two individuals except identical twins have the same DNA, Jeffreys believed that it would be possible to identify a person by DNA alone. In

The Blooding, an account of the Narborough murders, author Joseph Wambaugh recounts Jeffreys's certainty about the accuracy of DNA fingerprints. According to Wambaugh Jeffreys claimed:

> You would have to look for one part in a million million million million million before you would find one pair with the same genetic fingerprint, and with a world population of only five billion it can be categorically said that a genetic fingerprint is individually specific and that any pattern, excepting identical twins, does not belong to anyone on the face of this planet who ever has been or ever will be.[2]

Jeffreys chose the term *genetic fingerprinting* deliberately because he was certain that DNA fingerprinting would have important applications in police science, just as traditional fingerprinting had changed forensics in the nineteenth century.

The structure of DNA

Jeffreys's work was an outgrowth of one of the most important discoveries ever made in molecular biology. Thirty years earlier, in 1953, James Watson, a twenty-three-year-old American, and Francis Crick, a thirty-five-year-old Englishman, who worked together at Cambridge University in England, had announced to the world that they had unraveled the structure of the DNA molecule.

Crick, Watson, and other biologists had known for a long time that the nucleus of a cell contains its chromosomes, which act like a package of instructions that tell each cell what its role is and how to organize itself into a living creature. Every living plant or animal has chromosomes. Humans have forty-six, arranged in twenty-three pairs. The chromosomes contain the hereditary information that is passed from the mother and father to the child. Chromosomes consist of proteins and DNA. Watson and Crick discovered that DNA is formed by two winding strands that wrap around each other like a spiral ladder with 3 billion rungs. These rungs are composed of four chemicals called bases: adenine (A), thymine (T), guanine (G), and cytosine (C). The bases are always paired: each A is linked to a T, and each C is connected to a G. Watson and Crick immediately recognized the importance of understanding this structure. Watson, in his book *DNA: The Secret of Life*, wrote:

> DNA, as Crick and I appreciated, holds the very key to the nature of living things. It stores the hereditary information that is passed on from one generation to the next, and it orchestrates the incredibly complex world of the cell. Figuring out its 3-D structure—the molecule's architecture—would, we hoped, provide a glimpse of what Crick referred to only half-jokingly as "the secret of life."[3]

Watson and Crick knew that their discovery would have far-reaching effects in biology, chemistry, and medicine. But not even they predicted how this discovery would eventually wind its way into the field of criminal science.

Why is the structure of this molecule so important? The individual strands of DNA are so tiny that 5 million would fit through the eye of a needle. The twisting turns of this double-helix molecule cause it to coil up tightly inside the nucleus of each cell. The length of DNA in a single human cell is about one foot. Since each human being is composed of about 100 trillion specialized cells, the DNA strands in one human body would stretch to the sun and back one hundred times. The structure of DNA allows it to hold the vast amounts of information needed to program each of these cells to perform its unique and necessary function.

Since all human beings share most of the same features such as hands, feet, liver, heart, and lungs, huge chunks of DNA are the same in every human. In fact, human beings have 99.9 percent of their DNA in common. Small lengths of that molecule called polymorphisms, however, vary from person to person. For example, where one person might have an A, another person might have a G. These polymorphisms were considered unimportant at first, since they did not appear to be involved in any of the crucial directions to the cells. But it turned out that polymorphisms were the key to what made each person unique. Jeffreys noticed that in these polymorphic segments, the pattern of

A:T and C:G base pairs repeated over and over again. He found that he could analyze the polymorphisms using a process called RFLP analysis. It was given that name because a special chemical called a restriction enzyme is used to cut the DNA into small fragment lengths to analyze the polymorphisms. By then attaching a radioactive molecule to the segment being analyzed, Jeffreys found that he could x-ray the segment of DNA. The A:T and C:G pattern in each person's DNA then showed up on the X-ray like a code, almost like a bar code on packages in the grocery store. And most important for solving crimes, no two individuals except identical twins have the exact same code.

Two years after the first Narborough murder and a year before the second, Jeffreys was interviewed by the *Leicester Mercury* and concluded, "This new technique could mean a breakthrough in many areas, including the identification of a criminal from a small sample of blood at the scene of a crime."[4] Jeffreys was convinced that if skin cells, blood cells, or semen cells could be found at the scene of a crime, the unique DNA in those cells would lead to the culprit, and that crime could be solved.

A new mystery

Though Jeffreys used his technique for the first time to determine paternity in an immigration case in England, he was waiting for the opportunity to use DNA fingerprinting to solve a crime. He soon had the chance. When the police sent him semen and blood samples to analyze from the two rapes and murders in nearby Narborough, he had some shocking news for the Narborough police. Just as they suspected, the two girls had indeed been raped and murdered by the same man. But that man was not Richard Buckland, their primary suspect and the man who had confessed to the murder of Dawn Ashworth.

To find the real killer, the police asked all the men who lived or worked in the vicinity of the three neighboring villages to voluntarily submit blood or saliva samples for testing. They used traditional blood typing to eliminate anyone who had a different blood type than the murderer. The remaining 10 percent of the samples were subjected to Jeffreys's new DNA fingerprinting process. As each male villager was ruled out as a suspect, the community became more anxious and the authorities more desperate to nab the killer. Then, one day, a young baker named Ian Kelly was overheard in the local pub telling friends that he had been persuaded by his buddy Colin Pitchfork to take the test in his name. Pitchfork had claimed that he was too afraid of needles to take the test himself. Once they knew that, the

English geneticist Alec Jeffreys devised the DNA fingerprinting process in the 1980s.

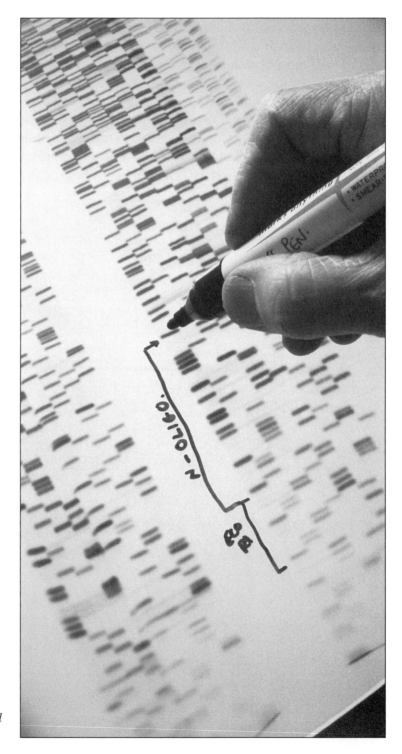

A researcher labels genetic code on a DNA X-ray. Forensic investigators use such code in order to link suspects with criminal acts.

police arrested Pitchfork and tested his DNA. Pitchfork's DNA matched the DNA evidence found on both Lynda Mann and Dawn Ashworth. Faced with the scientific truth, he confessed to the murders and was sentenced to life in prison in 1988. DNA had lived up to its promise. It had proved its power to law enforcement agencies around the world. It had both exonerated an innocent man and led to the conviction of a guilty one. Forensic science would never be the same.

Problems with the new DNA test

The initial success of DNA fingerprinting was hailed by many. It promised to be a flawless system of identification, and one that guaranteed objectivity. Now, many thought, if biological evidence could be collected, innocent suspects would not spend time in prison for crimes they had not committed. And those who were actually guilty of crimes where biological evidence could be found would not escape the punishments they deserved. But, despite its promise, early DNA testing had limitations to overcome and skeptics who needed to be convinced.

RFLP testing, though highly accurate, had some practical problems that made it difficult to use in some criminal cases. It took a lot of time—often months—and required a large sample of fluid or tissue. Sometimes, all that was available at a crime scene was a tiny speck of evidence. Barry Scheck explains in the book *Actual Innocence* how it was not always realistic to expect there to be enough DNA to test at every crime scene. As he says, "The problem with the DNA fingerprint test known as RFLP was that it could work only when there was a lot of DNA available. That was fine in the laboratory. But in the messy reality of crime scenes, DNA can be a scarce commodity."[5] Sometimes there might be enough DNA to complete one series of RFLP tests, but not enough left over to repeat the tests if necessary. Also, since RFLP involved attaching a radioactive molecule to the DNA, some scientists were reluctant to use it. Too much exposure to radioactive substances can be dangerous to humans.

Another early problem that surfaced with RFLP was that of its supposed objectivity. DNA matches are always expressed in probabilities rather than absolute certainties. In the early days of genetic fingerprinting, there were no standards for calculating those probablities. Defense attorneys argued with prosecutors who claimed that DNA matches between crime scene evidence and suspects were unquestionable. Watson explains in his book *DNA: The Secret of Life* how challenging it could be to determine DNA matches when the technology depended on RFLPs: "In this method, the DNA fingerprint appears as a series of bands on an X-ray film. If bands produced by the crime scene DNA were not identical to those produced by the suspects, just how much difference could be legitimately tolerated before one had to exclude the possibility of a match? Or how same does 'the same' have to be?"[6] These questions would have to be addressed before the U.S. criminal justice system would wholeheartedly embrace the new technology.

However, in spite of these early questions, law enforcement agencies in the United States were eager to try DNA fingerprinting to help solve crimes. The opportunity presented itself almost immediately in Florida the year after Colin Pitchfork murdered Dawn Ashworth in England. A series of break-ins, rapes, and robberies had been plaguing the city of Orlando. When the police arrested Tommy Lee Andrews for a different crime, they discovered that his DNA matched the DNA collected from one of the rape victims. At his trial, two geneticists testified for the prosecution. One was from Lifecodes, the first lab in the United States to do DNA analysis for criminal investigations, and the other came from the prestigious Massachusetts Institute of Technology (MIT). They agreed that the DNA belonged to Andrews and that his DNA profile could be found in only one in 10 billion individuals. On November 6, 1987, the circuit court in Orange County, Florida, convicted Andrews of rape, and he was sentenced to twenty-two years in prison. This was the first case in the United States in which DNA evidence was used to convict a criminal.

Shortly after the conviction of Tommy Lee Andrews, DNA was put to the test again. This time, it almost did not pass. David Rivera returned home from work in the Bronx in New York one evening to find that his pregnant common-law wife, Vilma Ponce, and their two-year-old daughter, Natasha, had been violently murdered. Though police suspected Rivera at first, after a monthlong investigation, they arrested the building handyman, Joseph Castro. While interviewing him, a police detective noticed a bloodstain on Castro's watch. Detectives sent the watch to the Lifecodes laboratory in Westchester, New York. The lab reported that the DNA on Castro's watch belonged to the victim, Vilma Ponce. Castro's fate seemed sealed. But then, Eric Lander, a scientist from MIT, challenged the scientist from Lifecodes.

During a 1987 homicide trial, researcher Eric Lander testified that a laboratory had tainted DNA evidence crucial to the case.

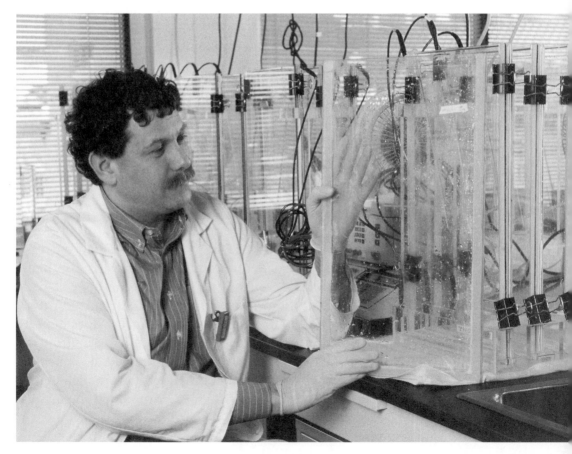

Lander argued that Lifecodes had used sloppy technique in the lab. He also claimed that misleading statistics overstated the likelihood of a DNA match between the blood on the watch and that of the victim. The judge, convinced that the DNA results could not be trusted, excluded them as evidence. The case against Castro, though, was compelling enough without the DNA that he eventually pleaded guilty to the two murders anyway in exchange for a lighter sentence. After he was sentenced, more tests were conducted that verified that the DNA on Castro's watchband did belong to the victim.

The Castro case represented a turning point for DNA evidence. It was now clear that legal standards for both laboratory procedures and statistics needed to be established before DNA evidence would have universal credibility. Everyone agreed that this fledgling technology could not afford another close call without risking a giant setback in its acceptance as a crime-fighting tool.

A major stumbling block in the ability to test DNA evidence was overcome in the late 1980s when scientists realized that they could take a technique that was being used in medical science and apply it to criminal investigations. A few years earlier, Kary Mullis, a chemist, figured out how to take a small piece of DNA, copy it millions of times, and then run the tests on the copies. Mullis called his process polymerase chain reaction (PCR) because an enzyme called a polymerase is used to cause a chain reaction that produces millions of identical copies of a piece of DNA. PCR was an improvement over RFLP because it became possible to take the tiniest bit of evidence—even a single cell—and copy the genetic information from the nucleus over and over until there was enough to test. The PCR process does not rely on X-rays, so it has the extra benefit of not requiring the use of radioactive materials. Even Mullis did not realize at first that his idea would have important applications in fighting crime. But in 1988, PCR provided the critical evidence in the first DNA exoneration of an innocent man in the United States.

Gary Dotson had served eight years of a twenty-five-to-fifty-year sentence for rape in Chicago, but he had never stopped proclaiming his innocence. When he heard about the DNA work of Dr. Jeffreys in England, his lawyers arranged to send the semen evidence from his trial to England for an RFLP test. But by then, there was insufficient evidence for the RFLP. The sample was then sent to San Francisco to be subjected to the newer PCR test, which confirmed Dotson's innocence. He was freed from prison.

PCR changed the scope of physical evidence. Prosecutors build their cases with many kinds of evidence, but it is the physical evidence that is often crucial to solving a crime. Paul L. Kirk explains the importance of physical evidence in his book *The Art and Science of Criminal Investigation:* "[Physical evidence] is evidence that does not forget. It is not confused by the excitement of the moment. It is not absent because human witnesses are. It cannot perjure itself; it cannot be wholly absent. Only its interpretation can err. Only human failure to find it, study and understand it, can diminish its value."[7]

DNA evidence is physical evidence on the molecular level. When PCR arrived on the scene as a new weapon in the arsenal of criminal investigation, it meant that the physical evidence left at or taken from a crime scene could now be as small as a single cell. A skin cell found beneath a victim's fingernail, semen stains or bloodstains, saliva residue, even a hair could now be used to identify a specific individual. Microscopic evidence now had enough power to determine with near absolute certainty whether or not an individual had been at the scene of certain crimes. Its power in the criminal justice system was steadily growing. But there was still another major obstacle to overcome.

Convincing the courts

As convincing as DNA fingerprinting could be, it was useless as evidence unless it was accepted by the courts as testimony. New breakthroughs in science are often slow to be accepted by the court system. Court decisions

Chemist Kary Mullis perfected a testing process in which even a single cell of DNA could be accurately analyzed.

can change people's lives forever, so new kinds of evidence must be proven trustworthy before juries can be asked to use them to make life-changing judgments. Since scientists are the only witnesses permitted to express opinions as well as facts in their testimony, those opinions can sway a jury. In 1993, the U.S. Supreme Court decided how to approach new scientific information. In a case known as *Daubert v. Merrell Dow Pharmaceuticals*, the Supreme Court adopted the Federal Rules of Evidence. This ensured that scientific information used as evidence in a case had first been published in respected scientific journals. The new Federal Rules of Evidence also required that the rates of error be acknowledged so that juries could judge whether the science being used as testimony was open at all to interpretation. This decision helped clear the way for DNA evidence in the courts. The force of this new DNA technology began to be felt more intensely as prosecutors and defense attorneys honed their skills at using it to further their causes.

There is no escape from DNA evidence. Believed to be individually specific, it has the power to point its genetic finger at the culprit—overriding confessions, accusations, suspicions, and even eyewitness accounts. In the space of less than twenty years, DNA technology has revolutionized crime fighting. DNA has given crime fighters the power to overcome human tendencies to deny responsibility, hide from the law, run from captivity, and claim innocence despite guilt. DNA has the power to unpeel the truth from layers of deceit. As the methods of DNA testing become increasingly accurate, it can truly be said that there is no hiding from genetics.

2

Convicting the Guilty

IN THE LAST decade of the twentieth century, DNA evidence was used with increasing frequency to link criminals with their crimes. The success of this tool of criminal justice also fueled its continuing development. Law enforcement officials became more skillful at negotiating the twists and turns of DNA evidence. By the end of the decade, DNA information was computerized and standardized throughout the United States, making it hard to escape its reach. Today DNA is an indispensable tool for solving crimes both old and new.

DNA gains acceptance

With each new success, DNA identification gained acceptance. By 1992, the credibility of DNA evidence was so strong that a rapist was convicted even though the victim insisted that her attacker was someone else. Carol Sanders, then twenty-eight, lived with her seven-year-old daughter in Baltimore, Maryland. One hot summer night in 1990, Sanders was awakened by an attack in the early morning hours. Since a pillowcase was drawn over her face, she could not see the man who was assaulting her, but she was positive that she recognized the voice and manner of her former boyfriend, John Davis. Since she and Davis had lived together, it was hard to imagine that she could be mistaken. But Davis had an alibi supported by his mother. He claimed he was home sleeping at the time of the attack. He offered to take a DNA test to prove his innocence.

When detectives arrived to take Davis's blood, Davis told them that he believed the actual rapist was Gregory Ritter, an acquaintance of Carol Sanders's roommate. When the DNA results from Davis's test proved that he was innocent, Baltimore prosecutor Scott Shellenberger was stunned. He had no choice but to release Davis from custody. Even though Sanders continued to insist that Davis was her rapist, the prosecutors based their decision to free Davis on DNA evidence alone. In his book *And the Blood Cried Out*, Harlan Davis explains Shellenberger's view: "DNA testing cannot be a one-way street, held out by prosecutors as conclusive evidence only when they like the results it yields."[8] The police now had no choice but to continue their search for Sanders's attacker.

On January 25, 1991, the police were authorized to extract Ritter's blood for DNA testing. The results proved the truth of Davis's accusations. There was no doubt that Ritter was the rapist. As Harlan Levy explains: "The prosecution was now in an odd position. The DNA results implicated Ritter, as did other facts. But the victim still maintained that Davis was the man who raped her. DNA or no DNA, she insisted it had been Davis."[9]

The silent testimony of a DNA test, however, proved more compelling than the determined insistence of the victim. Ritter was eventually sentenced to forty years in prison for the rape of Carol Sanders. The doubts and uncertainties surrounding DNA fingerprints were fading. In the last decade of the twentieth century, the criminal justice system came to depend more and more heavily on this genetic identification system.

Shortly after the conviction of Ritter for the nighttime attack on Sanders, the attention of the entire nation was focused on the use of DNA evidence when the World Trade Center in New York City was bombed on February 26, 1993. This was the first major act of international terrorism on American soil. Six people were killed and over one thousand were injured. Since the yellow van that carried the explosives was blasted into thousands of unrecognizable pieces, it seemed likely that the terrorists might escape detection.

A week later, the *New York Times* received an anonymous letter explaining that the explosion was a response to American political, economic, and military support for Israel. Two men were subsequently arrested for the bombing: Mohammed Salameh, an unemployed construction worker, and Nidal Ayyad, a chemical engineer who had graduated from Rutgers University in New Jersey. The evidence against Salameh was gathered by old-fashioned detective work that linked some intact pieces of the van to the Ryder rental agency where Salameh had rented the van. But Ayyad was identified with a modern twist when the envelope bearing the letter to the *Times* was subjected to PCR. Ayyad, Salameh's friend, had licked the envelope, and the incriminating DNA was there to prove it.

The continuing acceptance of DNA evidence also fueled advances in its development as a crime-fighting tool. Criminal investigators figured out how to take a method of DNA analysis that had been developed to study the bones of ancient Neanderthals and apply it to police science. In very old evidence in which the cells' nuclei have deteriorated beyond the reach of the standard DNA test, scientists discovered that it was still possible to analyze the tiny loop of DNA contained in the mitochondria—part of the cell outside the nucleus. Using PCR to copy the mitochondrial DNA (mtDNA) allowed criminal scientists to salvage old evidence for genetic fingerprinting. MtDNA tests can also be used to analyze hair fragments that lack roots and so do not have cells that contain a nucleus. Before mtDNA analysis, hair was often identified microscopically using factors such as color, texture, and amount of curl, all of which proved to be highly subjective and unreliable. In fact, when wrongful convictions were later studied, 35 percent of those convictions included testimony about hair analysis that was later proved inaccurate by mtDNA. MtDNA analysis is also used on bones, teeth, and fingernails.

Although there are some instances in which mtDNA can be very useful to investigators, it also has some limitations in police science. MtDNA is inherited only from the

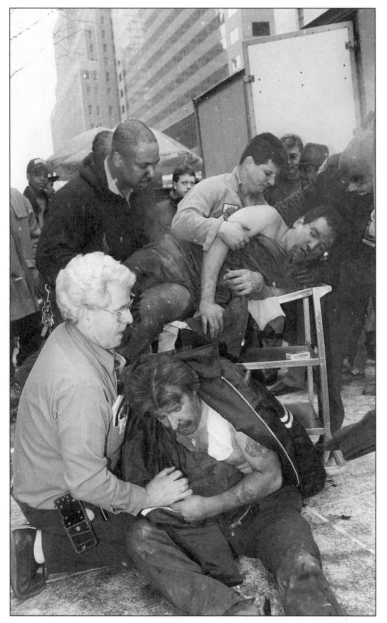

Medics attend to victims of the 1993 World Trade Center bombing. One of the bombers, Nidal Ayyad, was convicted with DNA collected from an envelope he had licked.

mother, unlike DNA in the cell nucleus that comes from both parents. This means that anyone related to the same mother, no matter how distant that relationship may be, will share common base patterns in their mtDNA. This can be helpful in figuring out whether victims are related, but it

A U.S. Marshal leads convicted terrorist Nidal Ayyad (right) from the courthouse.

also means that there are many people with the same mtDNA. DNA from the nucleus is specific to only one individual on the face of the earth.

DNA from surprising sources

As DNA technology progressed, even nonhuman DNA found its use in human jurisprudence. At Prince Edward Island, Canada, on the eastern seaboard, a woman disappeared from her home in 1997. At first, the only evidence was a brown leather jacket stained with blood found in a plastic bag in the woods near her home. The lining of the jacket was littered with white cat hairs. After her body was discovered, the woman's common-law husband was arrested and the blood and cat hairs subjected to a powerful PCR test. The blood belonged to the victim. The DNA on the cat hairs matched the DNA that belonged to Snowball, the suspect's parents' white cat. The cat hairs in the bag snagged the killer.

Plant DNA can point a guilty finger too. A murdered woman was discovered in the early 1990s in the Arizona desert near a group of paloverde trees. Two paloverde seed pods found in the bed of a truck driven by Mark Bogan added to police suspicion that Bogan had killed the woman. DNA proved that the seed pods in the truck matched the seed pods at the scene of the crime. The jury

A Virginia police officer gathers blood samples from a crime scene. Virginia was the first state to require certain types of offenders to submit DNA samples.

found this evidence persuasive enough to convict Bogan of murder, and in 1995, an appeals court upheld the conviction.

Even human DNA sometimes shows up in unlikely places. Usually DNA is collected from blood evidence, which is found at 60 percent of murders, assaults, and batteries. Or DNA can be gathered from saliva or semen, in the case of sexual assault. Sometimes, DNA is collected from skin cells scraped from under the fingernails of victims who have clawed desperately at their attackers. In an unusual twist, human DNA discovered in the beak of a white-crested cockatoo named Bird was a key piece of evidence in the conviction of Daniel Torres for the murder of Kevin Butler in 2003. According to the *San Diego Union Tribune*, prosecutors explained how the big white bird ended up with human DNA in its beak: During a struggle, the bird "swooped down on the attackers, clawed at their skin and pecked at their heads."[10] Torres's skin cells, extracted from the bird's beak with their incriminating DNA, were presented as evidence at the trial. Bird suffered the same fate as his owner. The cockatoo was stabbed to death by Torres in the kitchen of Butler's home.

Computer matches and DNA data banks

Although DNA was being discovered in some improbable places and the technology to identify it was increasingly sophisticated, the means to link DNA evidence to specific individuals were still primitive. When the case of Tommy Lee Andrews came to trial in Florida in 1987, a uniform system for saving DNA information did not exist, which made it difficult to connect individuals to their crimes. A computer database was needed that would allow DNA test results from individuals convicted of certain crimes to be matched with DNA from the scenes of unsolved crimes.

In 1989, Virginia became the first state to pass laws requiring certain types of offenders to submit DNA samples for data bank purposes. One year later, Virginia laws were expanded to require all felons to provide samples.

Virginia's data bank proved useful a few years ago when a serial rapist was terrorizing a neighborhood in Charlottesville. Investigators were frustrated in their search for the attacker since no one could identify him. All they could do was gather DNA evidence from the rapes and hope that they could connect the DNA to a criminal whose DNA information already existed in the state database. They finally found a match. In 2000, the state DNA database matched the evidence from several crime scenes to one man, Shannon Malenowski. After his arrest, the attacks stopped. Applauding the power of the database, a Charlottesville police lieutenant, Chip Harding, explained: "This was a case where the computer saw the suspect and the eyewitness did not."[11]

Although Virginia was the first state to establish a DNA data bank for felons, by 1998 every state in the country had

A state forensic scientist prepares a DNA sample for testing. By 1998 every U.S. state had its own DNA data bank.

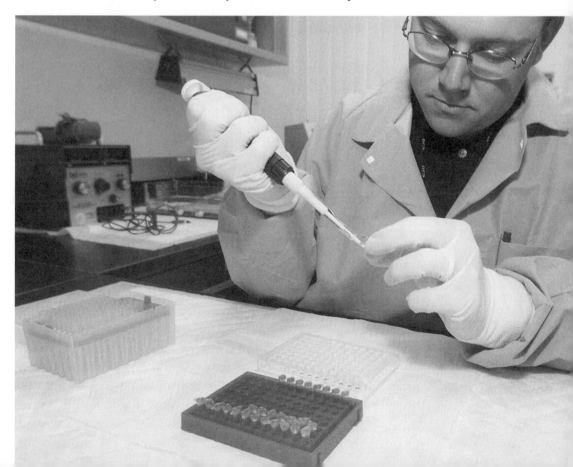

passed a law establishing its own data bank, though laws in each state still differ about who is required to submit DNA samples. Every state requires DNA from convicted sex offenders. Some states bank DNA only from those who have been convicted of felonies, while others require DNA samples upon arrest for any offense.

Individual state data banks present challenges to law enforcement since many criminals are transient and move frequently from one state to another. In the first interstate hit using state data banks, investigators were able to link four rape cases in Florida in 1997 to the same individual. When a search of the Florida database was unsuccessful, police requested a DNA database search from two nearby states: Virginia and Florida. One day later, Florida detectives received a call from Virginia authorities. The mystery DNA belonged to Mark Daigle, a convicted Virginia burglar.

By 1990, the FBI had established its own federal database, known as CODIS: Combined DNA Index System. CODIS contained over 1 million DNA fingerprints by the middle of 2002. Of these stored DNA fingerprints, 978,000 belonged to convicted offenders and almost 36,000 were crime scene evidence from unsolved cases. In order for the system to work efficiently, all forensic laboratories who participate in CODIS must use compatible systems so the data can be compared. The Violent Crime Control and Law Enforcement Act of 1994 was enacted to provide federal support to state and local law enforcement agencies so they could participate in this federal DNA database.

The improved ability to store DNA information for later searches added to the power of this technology that was revolutionizing crime fighting. Once databases were in place, DNA could unravel old mysteries, revealing new endings and providing victims and their families with long-lost peace of mind. Harlan Levy explained the power of DNA to unearth the past: "The new truth machine was also a time machine. It made it possible to look into the past, to reveal the truth about events that took place years ago."[12]

One old case that was given new life by CODIS involved a young woman named Donna Hooker, who was twenty-one in 1978 when she was raped, strangled, and dumped in a field near her home in Sacramento, California. When her case came up for review, old evidence was run through CODIS. It matched the DNA of Norman Whitehorn, who was already in prison serving time on a federal weapons charge. ABC News reported that DNA had reignited a case long ago given up for dead: "Now this 'cold' case is hot again," Sacramento district attorney Jan Scully told ABC. "In this day and age, people can change the color of their eyes and other physical descriptors, but they can't change their DNA."[13] Whitehorn has been charged with Hooker's murder and may be facing the death penalty.

Collecting DNA

As DNA evidence became more familiar to the general public, it became more difficult to convince suspects to voluntarily submit their DNA for testing. No longer would all suspects willingly extend an arm for a blood sample or open their mouths for a cheek swab so their DNA could be tested. Police investigators began resorting to subtler methods of gathering the DNA they needed to help solve crimes. Police in Seattle linked a man to the murder of a thirteen-year-old girl after he licked the return envelope to a bogus invitation they mailed to him. He thought he was being invited to join a class-action lawsuit on behalf of people who had been overcharged on parking tickets. Instead, his saliva, surreptitiously collected, was matched with DNA from the crime.

James Alan Fox, a professor of criminal justice at Northeastern University in Chicago, wrote a book about the murders of five University of Florida students in 1990. He described how investigators checked the DNA of hundreds of people in that case as they searched for the murderer, often without them knowing: "We'd follow people as they went through Burger King, and pick up a straw they used for saliva. We'd go through their trash on the sidewalk. Not everybody we got DNA on even knew it."[14]

Police used DNA from saliva collected from a cigarette butt to arrest this man nearly thirty years after he allegedly murdered a local woman.

DNA from the trash also provided the evidence in an unusual case involving identical twins, the only people who share the exact same DNA fingerprint. This fact can sometimes present a special challenge to law enforcement. For years, police had been unsuccessful in solving the 1990 rape and murder of Laurie Colannino in Pinella, Florida. When the case was reopened, all the residents of Colannino's apartment complex who had lived there at the time of the murder were asked to submit to DNA tests, including one man, Brian Calzacorto, who refused. Police then approached his twin brother, Alfred, knowing their DNA would be the same. But Alfred also refused. So in August 2000, police staked out Brian's apartment and subjected some of his garbage, including used razor blades and old cigarette butts, to DNA tests. The DNA they found in the trash matched DNA deposited on the victim. The police then had to figure out which twin had deposited the DNA.

Brian's attorney insisted the DNA belonged to Alfred. But Alfred had an alibi. He was working twenty miles away in Tampa at the time of Colannino's attack. Brian was convicted and sentenced to life in prison for murder.

John Doe warrants

In a strategy that has gained popularity in recent years, police with DNA profiles but no matches have begun issuing so-called John Doe warrants. "John Doe" indicates that a person's real name is unknown. Suspects on these warrants are identified only by their unique genetic profiles. Once the DNA databases have been searched and a match has been established, the real name is substituted on the warrant and the suspect can be arrested. Paul Eugene Robinson, known as the "Second Story Rapist" for a series of rapes in Sacramento apartment houses in the mid-1990s, was the first suspect in the nation to be arrested under a John Doe warrant that identified him solely by his DNA

In 2001 Paul Eugene Robinson (left) became the first defendant in California to be convicted of rape based on a John Doe warrant.

In 2003 New York City mayor Michael Bloomberg announces the state's John Doe Indictment Project, designed to solve old sex crimes using DNA evidence.

fingerprint. The warrant was issued in 2000, just three days before the statute of limitations on one of his crimes was due to expire. A month after the warrant was issued, a state Department of Justice computer matched the DNA profile to Robinson. Robinson's conviction was the first in California based on a John Doe warrant. Robinson's attorney challenged the conviction, arguing that the warrant did not specifically name his client, but the judge upheld the ruling, remarking that: "DNA appears to be the best identifier of a person that we have."[15]

In New York City, officials have launched an ambitious plan to solve old sex crimes. Called the John Doe Indictment Project, investigators will review biological evidence from hundreds of unsolved crimes with the goal of developing DNA profiles on the attackers. They will then issue John Doe warrants. New York State law currently gives prosecutors ten years to find attackers and file charges before the statute of limitations makes prosecution impossible. Prosecutors in New York plan to begin by reviewing six hundred sex crimes from the mid-1990s in order to develop DNA profiles for those cases before the statutes of limitation run out. Officials there believe that the John Doe warrants will enable them to prosecute those crimes any time in the future. New York City mayor Michael Bloomberg explained how John Doe warrants advance the cause of criminal justice:

> One very simple goal is behind this strategy: stopping rapists from profiting from the statue of limitations. By indicting a rapist's DNA profile even before we know who he is, we can stop the clock on the statute of limitations. So on the day that we find out who that rapist is, whether it takes us 10 years, 20 years, 30 years or more, he will have his day in court.[16]

In a way, subjecting DNA information to databases containing millions of DNA profiles is not that different from testing the blood of every male in a community to find a rapist as police did in Narborough, England, twenty years ago. A database search is simply a dragnet of greater magnitude.

DNA is a tool that can pick out a suspect from a lineup of all the individuals that inhabit the earth. It is a powerful tool, but it cannot work alone. DNA is only one part of a system for finding suspects. In order to point its incriminating finger, DNA needs the muscle and bone of the street cops, the investigators, and the forensic experts in the crime lab. All these parts must work together to nab the bad guys. Skillfully wielded, DNA is a tool that can go far toward protecting the public.

3

Freeing the Innocent

IT IS HUMAN nature to feel a sense of urgency about figuring out exactly what happened and punishing someone when a violent crime has been committed against an innocent person. The founders of the United States government knew that when they built protections for ordinary citizens into the Constitution. Anyone accused of a crime, for instance, is guaranteed the right to an attorney—one who specializes in defending the accused. The defense attorney does not need to prove innocence. The defense attorney's job is solely to place a reasonable doubt in the minds of the jurors that prevents them from finding a suspect guilty. But sometimes, even with guaranteed rights and Constitutional safeguards, innocent people are still convicted and sent to prison—even sentenced to die.

When DNA appeared on the criminal justice scene, it gave defense attorneys a new tool. Over the period of just a few years, this molecule, with its ability to identify who was or was not at the scene of a crime, gained immense power. Prisoners serving time for crimes they had not committed had renewed hope of escaping punishments they knew they did not deserve. Arthur Eisenberg, director of the DNA Identity Laboratory at the University of North Texas Health Science Center, explained the importance of using DNA to prove innocence: "Using DNA to exonerate innocent suspects and prisoners is just as important as finding criminals,"[17] he said. DNA was the new key to unlocking prison doors, even some that had slammed shut many years before. Once it became evident that innocent people were imprisoned for crimes they had not committed, controversy rippled around the country concerning the death penalty, the most serious punishment of all.

Reasons for wrongful convictions

There are many reasons that someone who is innocent is convicted of a crime and ends up in prison. When wrongful convictions were studied in the late 1990s, 22 percent were found to be based on false confessions. The pressure surrounding the search for the perpetrator of a violent crime is

A defense attorney submits a bloodstained jacket as evidence at trial. In addition to helping convict criminals, DNA is also used to establish innocence.

often intense. Sometimes, suspects who are subjected to hours of questioning by detectives skilled at interrogation will confess even though they are innocent. Sometimes innocent suspects, who may be young or vulnerable in some other way, will agree to the possibility that they were involved in a crime while claiming to have forgotten most of the details. Fear often plays a part in false confessions. The threat of punishment for a more serious crime can sometimes convince a suspect to confess to a crime that appears to carry less severe consequences.

By far the most common cause of wrongful imprisonment, however, is eyewitness error. Even though testimony by eyewitnesses and victims is very convincing to juries, many studies confirm that the human memory is extremely unreliable, especially when the circumstances are stressful, as they are during the commission of a crime. Barry Scheck describes the unreliability of eyewitness accounts in the book *Actual Innocence:* "A thousand people can witness a crime and recall a thousand different details."[18] Studies have demonstrated that 82 percent of wrongful convictions could be blamed at least in part on mistaken identity by eyewitnesses.

Sometimes accusers deliberately send police in the wrong direction, either to protect themselves or someone else. One type of accusation engaged in by prison inmates is known as "informing" or "jailhouse snitching." This is the practice of one inmate exchanging information about another inmate in exchange for the promise of reduced time in prison. The inmate known as the "snitch" reports to prison authorities and may later testify in court that he or she has overheard another inmate confess to a particular crime. Depending on the outcome, the snitch may be rewarded for the information with months or years shaved off his or her prison sentence.

Though the reasons for wrongful conviction are varied and often complex, DNA has become a valuable tool to help the wrongfully convicted prove their innocence. When Gary Dotson was exonerated by DNA evidence in 1988 after his conviction for rape, his accuser, Cathleen

Crowell Webb, admitted that she had invented the rape story to protect her reputation. The sixteen-year-old girl later told investigators that she was afraid that her foster parents would be angry with her if she became pregnant after having sex with her boyfriend. So she ripped her own clothing and accused Dotson of raping her.

DNA can also overcome the convincing claim of false confessions. Four teenagers later regretted confessing to the murder of Lori Roscetti, a medical student who was killed in Illinois one night in 1986 on her way home from the library. Four young boys—Omar Saunders, Marcellius Bradford, Larry Ollins, and his cousin Calvin Ollins— were arrested and soon admitted participating in the crime. Bradford and Calvin were fourteen years old. Bradford explained later that he confessed and testified against the others to save himself from a life sentence. Years later he told how much he regretted that decision, claiming: "I thought about it every day. I'm going to skateboard into hell."[19] Calvin said that he confessed because the police promised him that he could go home if he admitted his part in the murder. Although DNA from the four teenagers did not match the DNA collected from the crime scene, their confessions sealed their fates. Three of the boys received life sentences since they were too young to receive the death penalty in Illinois. Bradford exchanged his testimony against the others for a shorter sentence.

Fifteen years later the real killer confessed. Kathleen Zellner, a public defender in Illinois, spent fifty thousand dollars of her own money and volunteered eight hundred hours of time on the case. She discovered clothing belonging to Roscetti that was stained with DNA evidence and had not been analyzed in the original investigation. The results of the DNA tests on that evidence unequivocally cleared the four young men.

Kirk Bloodsworth was the victim of mistaken identification by several eyewitnesses. When the state of Maryland sentenced Bloodsworth to die in 1985 for the rape and murder of nine-year-old Dawn Hamilton, DNA fingerprinting was still brand new. Among the eyewitnesses who testified that they could identify Bloodsworth were two young boys: Chris, who was ten years old, and Jackie, who was almost eight. The two friends had been fishing at a pond outside rural Baltimore one summer when a man walked by. The boys called out to him and offered to show him the turtle they had found in the pond. The man seemed friendly, and when Dawn Hamilton, a friend of the boys, walked by looking for her cousin, the man offered to help her find the girl. A woman working in her yard saw the young girl walk by with a man. Five hours later, Dawn's body was discovered facedown in the bushes. Her skull was crushed and she had been raped. The two boys provided details of the man's face to a police artist. When the resulting composite sketch appeared in the *Baltimore Evening Sun*, another eyewitness told authorities that the sketch reminded her of a man who worked at a furniture importing store not far from the murder scene. All she knew was that the man's name was Kirk.

Although the testimony of each of the eyewitnesses was open to question and Bloodsworth never stopped claiming his innocence, he was convicted of murder and sentenced to die. But nine years later, when DNA was firmly established as a credible means of identification, the victim's underwear, with its tiny preserved semen stain, provided enough evidence to free him. In 1993, Bloodsworth became the first person in the nation convicted in a death penalty case to be exonerated by DNA. Barry Scheck explains in *Actual Innocence* how DNA rescued Bloodsworth:

> A semen stain the size of a dime saved Kirk Bloodsworth. He owes his life to the depravity of a murderer. Suppose the killer of Dawn Hamilton had "merely" murdered her, and not added sexual assault to his crime; there would have been no semen on Dawn's panties to find, no sperm cells barcoded with the murderer's DNA and not Kirk Bloodsworth's. But for that, the state of Maryland, under authority granted it by the U.S. Supreme Court, would have murdered an innocent man.[20]

In Bloodsworth's case, DNA not only exonerated an innocent man, it also identified the real culprit. In the spring

of 2003, a forensic biologist studying the old case found stains on a sheet that had not been analyzed. Results run through the national DNA database identified the real rapist ten years after the crime had been committed.

Larry Ollins, Omar Saunders, and Calvin Ollins (L to R) celebrate their release from a life sentence for murder after new DNA evidence exonerated them.

The Innocence Project

Two young attorneys who worked together at Legal Aid in New York City were increasingly disturbed by cases like Bloodsworth's in which innocent people were convicted of crimes and sentenced to prison. They were determined to find out how this happened and to help these innocent victims of the criminal justice system navigate the complex maze out of prison. In 1992, Barry Scheck and Peter

Kirk Bloodworth was the first prisoner in the United States to be freed from death row on the basis of DNA evidence.

Neufeld, old friends and colleagues, created the Innocence Project, a nonprofit legal clinic based at the Benjamin N. Cardozo School of Law in New York. Their goal was to right the wrongs they were finding in their work as public defenders. The Innocence Project handles cases in which DNA evidence can provide absolute proof of innocence. Neufeld had already developed a reputation in the early 1990s as an expert on scientific evidence.

Scheck and Neufeld decided to publicize their success in a case in which a truck driver was proven innocent of rape after spending eleven years in prison. Sensitive DNA tests, unavailable when the man had been convicted in the early 1980s, had provided absolute certainty of his innocence. Scheck and Neufeld described the firestorm generated by the news:

> Word of this new DNA test moved from cell to cell block, from tier to prison yard, from the weekend visiting room to the chartered bus rides home, from cities to states, coast to

coast. Innocent people in jails lunged at this story. They wrote to Barry and Peter and asked them to make it happen again. Other defense lawyers called to ask for help. So did mothers and fathers, brothers and sisters.[21]

The Innocence Project takes on only cases that involve biological evidence such as sperm, blood, saliva, skin, or hair. Cases are evaluated thoroughly beforehand to determine whether that DNA evidence can yield conclusive proof of innocence. Most of the cases are handled by law students whose work is supervised by practicing attorneys. The legal services are provided free of charge, but the DNA testing itself is paid for with private funds. The Innocence Project describes its mission to help innocent victims of the crminal justice system: "Most of our clients are poor, forgotten, and have used up all their legal avenues for relief. The hope they all have is that biological evidence from their cases still exists and can be subjected to DNA testing."[22]

Peter Neufeld (left) and Barry Scheck created New York's Innocence Project in 1992 to help free innocent convicts using DNA evidence.

The process of seeking postconviction exoneration begins when an attorney files an appeal called a writ of habeas corpus claiming that new evidence exists that will exonerate the inmate. All the old evidence surrounding the conviction is reviewed. Witnesses are interviewed again. Biological evidence such as DNA is tested or retested. Sometimes, investigators discover that old evidence was never tested for DNA. One difficulty is that defense attorneys do not have access to state and federal databases. This makes it hard to find alternate suspects. It generally takes from three to five years for the entire process of postconviction testing to be completed from the time a request is first received.

Despite the challenges, the Innocence Project at Cardozo has inspired dozens of similar undertakings around the country in the past decade. According to an article in the *Dallas Morning News* in June 2002, these all-volunteer coalitions are made up of police officers, investigative reporters, defense attorneys, students, and professors. Almost all of them depend on private donations. Only

Barry Scheck holds a client's hand as they wait for a new verdict. The Innocence Project has inspired similar efforts in other states.

California and New York provide some public funding. The California Innocence Project is based at California Western School of Law in San Diego. It has been involved in three case reviews with favorable results: two exonerations and one reduction in sentence, according to the *San Diego Union Tribune*. Commenting on the growth of the Innocence Projects in the country, Peter Neufeld told the Associated Press: "We started out with a very simple goal, and that is to walk innocent people out of prison. And what it has evolved into is nothing less than a new civil rights movement in this country."[23]

DNA with its ability to zero in on suspects and eliminate others has propelled these Innocence Projects and keeps them running. Keith Findley, the codirector of the Innocence Project at the University of Wisconsin, explained the role of DNA in their work: "The DNA cases have been really important for the innocence projects because they establish innocence with such scientific certainty."[24] As of October 2, 2003, the Innocence Project at the Cardozo Law School had proven that 138 convicted prisoners were actually innocent. Thousands of cases await evaluation.

Postconviction DNA testing

While the Innocence Projects and similar efforts around the country have demonstrated conclusively that mistakes are made and people are wrongfully convicted, there is ongoing debate about who should qualify for postconviction testing and for how long that testing should be made available to inmates. Prosecutors and district attorneys whose jobs depend on proving beyond a reasonable doubt that a suspect is guilty sometimes resist postconviction DNA testing. They believe that DNA tests alone are not proof of innocence. They argue that while the presence of DNA at a crime scene can be used to establish guilt, its absence does not necessarily prove innocence. Peter Roff, a political analyst, echoed the opinions of many opponents to postconviction DNA testing when he told United Press International: "It is the entire body of evidence that must be considered, not just the results of lab tests performed on old clothing. These DNA requests will tax the already overburdened legal system, depriving the victims and the wrongfully accused of their day in court in a timely manner."[25] Roff believes that postconviction testing wastes taxpayer money. There are other arguments against increasing the accessibility of postconviction DNA testing besides expense: Evidence from old trials is often difficult or impossible to locate, and the laboratories capable of performing DNA tests are overburdened enough by their current workloads.

Roff supports the decision of the Florida legislature, which decided in 2001 to give convicts two years to apply for postconviction DNA testing before permanently closing the door on that possibility. As of October 1, 2003, convicts could no longer request DNA testing after conviction. Jennifer Greenberg, a director of the Innocence Project in Florida, disagreed with the decision, saying: "There should be no statute of limitations on innocence."[26] Many other states, including Delaware, Michigan, New Mexico, Ohio, Oregon, and Washington, are also considering legislation that will effectively eliminate postconviction DNA testing.

Greenberg is not alone in her opinion. Former FBI director William S. Sessions argues that prosecutors have a moral and professional duty to seek the truth no matter how long it takes. In an article in the *Washington Post*, Sessions offered his views on postconviction DNA testing: "If it exonerates the defendant, then there is an opportunity to correct a tragic mistake and begin the search for the real criminal."[27]

In an effort to address the problem of wrongful convictions and make postconviction DNA testing more uniformly available, the Innocence Project has urged Congress to adopt federal legislation that would provide national access to postconviction DNA testing. In July 2003, Peter Neufeld testified before the House Judiciary Committee in support of a bill called *Advancing Justice Through DNA Technology Act*. This bill would grant any inmate convicted of a federal crime access to DNA testing to support a claim of innocence. The bill also encourages the states to adopt adequate measures to preserve evidence and make the postconviction DNA tests available. To support this legislation, the bill establishes the Kirk Bloodsworth Post-Conviction DNA Testing Program, which would provide $25 million to the states to defray the costs of postconviction testing.

DNA and the death penalty

Although Kirk Bloodsworth was the first death row inmate exonerated by DNA, he was not the last. Cases like Bloodsworth's, along with the increasing acceptance of DNA evidence, have added fuel to the heated debate about the death penalty. Both those who are in favor of the death penalty and those who oppose it use the possibility of scientific accuracy to give weight to their arguments. One governor, Mitt Romney of Massachusetts, assembled a council of experts in late 2003, including DNA specialists, to try to convince his state to reinstate the death penalty, which was abolished there in 1984. He said that he wants to put "science above all else," to guarantee that only the guilty will be executed: "I really am looking for a standard of certainty," he said. "That's why I've asked this panel of experts to determine if a legal and forensic standard can be crafted to assure us that only the guilty will suffer the death penalty. I believe it can be."[28] Romney believes that the majority of the public would favor the death penalty for the worst kinds of homicide if people could be assured that it was never administered unfairly or in error.

But death penalty opponents are still troubled by factors that they believe even the most finely crafted legislation cannot overcome. DNA testing can prove whether or not a suspect was present at the scene of a crime, but it tells nothing about many other factors that are considered critical in death penalty cases: motive, the presence of another suspect, the possibility of self-defense. Even if the forensic laboratories responsible for DNA tests operated completely independently of all police and government agencies, critics of the death penalty believe that it would still be impossible to eliminate the possiblity of human error from the testing procedure. James Alan Fox, a professor of criminal justice at Northeastern University, described that problem: "Science is performed by scientists and scientists are human beings, and they are not infallible. Science is irrefutable, but scientists can make mistakes."[29]

Illinois governor George Ryan was so troubled by these concerns that he imposed a moratorium on the death penalty in that state in 2000. Ryan explained his action by saying that he could not ignore the fact that 13 people on death row in Illinois were found to be innocent and released through DNA evidence, witnesses who changed their minds, and determined attorneys. In January 2003, Ryan, who was elected in 1998 as a death penalty supporter, made his final decision concerning the death row inmates in Illinois. Four of them were released from prison. The remaining 167 had their sentences commuted from death to life in prison. Opinions varied widely about the legality and ethics of Ryan's actions. The state attorney general challenged Ryan's decision in court to offer blanket clemency to condemned inmates. In January 2004, the Illinois Supreme Court upheld the governor's power to commute the sentences of everyone on death row. Others applauded the governor's actions. Ryan, sixty-nine, was nominated for the 2003 Nobel Peace Prize for his actions involving the death penalty in his state. No other state has announced plans to follow Ryan's example.

While decisions about using DNA evidence to support or refute the ethics of the death penalty remain unresolved, DNA continues to change the face of the criminal justice system. At the same time that police and attorneys have learned to use DNA to find the perpetrators of violent crimes, they have also come to depend on it to separate the innocent from the guilty. DNA evidence has given the criminal justice system both the weight of scientific accuracy and the knowledge of human fallibility. It is no longer enough to find and release individuals one by one who have been mistakenly convicted. It is also important to analyze how and why this happens so that it does not happen

again. DNA testing has opened a window into wrongful convictions. Now it is up to those who legislate the laws, those who practice the law, and those who enforce the law to study the causes and propose the remedies so that innocent people will not be convicted in the first place for crimes they did not commit.

Illinois governor George Ryan halted the death penalty in his state after DNA evidence proved thirteen death-row inmates were innocent.

4

Protecting Wildlife

DNA, THE MOLECULE whose twists and turns help solve crimes against humanity, has many roles in the world of wildlife protection too. Just as all humans have many of the same gene sequences, which determine basic body parts such as eyes, hair, skin, and hearts, each animal within any species has most of its DNA in common with every other member of that species. It is the differences, many of them quite subtle, that make each individual member of a species unique. But in wildlife law, the value of DNA often extends beyond the individual animal. DNA helps keep track of entire populations of animals that are threatened by hunting, fishing, and a black market for their smuggled body parts. DNA is the genetic tattletale that helps scientists and governments around the world keep these populations healthy.

Cracking cases of egg smugglers

Fighting illegal trade in wildlife is a constant battle worldwide. As species of birds and plants become rare and endangered, protecting them becomes increasingly crucial. It can mean the difference between their preservation and their extinction. DNA has given new strength to wildlife officials in Australia in their battle to prevent the illegal smuggling of rare birds. In recent years, illegal traffickers have begun smuggling the fertilized eggs of these birds and hatching them in incubators when the eggs are safely out of that country.

Eggs are an obvious choice for smugglers. A noisy bird gives itself away, making it difficult to hide, while eggs can be hidden and quietly transported to their ultimate destination. In one case in Australia, a woman was discovered with seven eggs hidden in her bra. As she was questioned by suspicious customs officials, she smashed the eggs. She insisted the broken yolks were merely pigeon eggs, which would have saved her from prosecution for the more serious offense of smuggling rare and endangered birds.

Customs officials turned to the Victorian Museum in Melbourne to help determine the species of the smashed eggs. Dr. Les Christidies, the museum's curator of birds, used the same DNA technology that police use to establish human identity. Christidies and his colleague, Dr. Janette Norman, first determined that all the eggs in the woman's bra belonged to the same species. The scientists then compared the DNA from the smashed egg membrane to the DNA database they were building from the museum's collection of seventy thousand bird specimens to identify exactly which species of bird had laid those eggs.

Wildlife forensics laboratories, such as the one in Ashland, Oregon (pictured), provide crucial DNA evidence for prosecution of crimes involving endangered species.

It took two weeks to find that the smuggled eggs were galahs, commonly known as rose-breasted cockatoos. "Rosies" are popular pets in Australia, but their export is severely limited, which makes them tempting to smuggle. As Norman explained in an interview with ABC News in Australia: "There's big, big money in smuggling. A single egg can be worth $50,000 if it's hatched and raised to an adult."[30]

Before customs began using DNA to nab bird smugglers, it could take up to six months to hatch an egg to determine its species. Since that first case, DNA has provided the evidence used to snare several bird smugglers in Australia. Officials there are compiling a national database of Australian birds to help contain this problem.

A forensic scientist autopsies a rare cat at the national laboratory in Oregon. The lab has been called wildlife's Scotland Yard.

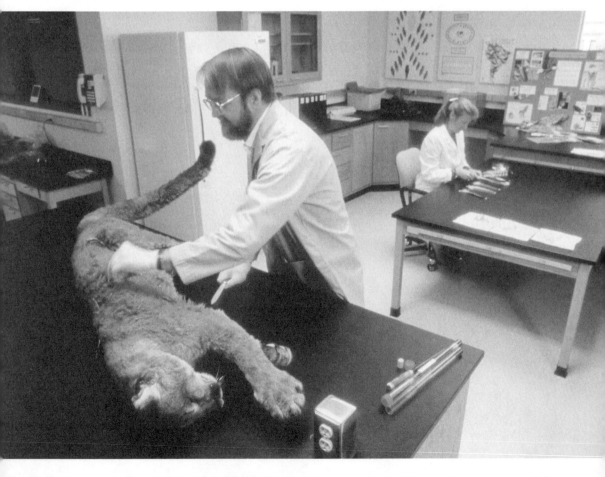

The National Fish and Wildlife Forensics Laboratory

Wildlife forensics in Australia and the world over are supported by the National Fish and Wildlife Forensics Laboratory in the United States. Until a few years ago, this federal facility located in Ashland, Oregon, was the only lab in the world that was devoted solely to solving crimes against wildlife. The lab works with federal agents around the country and the state fish and game commissions in all fifty states. It also provides forensic support to the 155 countries that agreed to the articles in the Convention on International Trade in Endangered Species of Wild Fauna and Flora (CITES) that was signed in 1975. The lab has been called the wild world's Scotland Yard, a reference to the famous police crime lab in London, England. The lab's work frequently involves using DNA to identify an animal's species. This information then aids police or other wildlife agents in determining which law has been broken and linking the crime to a human suspect. Ken Goddard, the lab's director, explained how the wildlife lab solves crimes:

> We use DNA as one of our tools to do two things that crime labs all do, whether they are a wildlife crime lab or a police crime lab. We identify evidence, and we attempt to link suspect, victim and crime scene together. It's also possible if we know enough about the DNA of the species in question that we can say the head on the wall matches the gut pile at a certain place. That animal and no other animal in the world.[31]

In this way the wildlife lab functions exactly like a human police crime lab.

DNA evidence plays a part in 15 to 20 percent of the lab's cases. And just like its human counterpart, animal DNA can unravel old mysteries that have long resisted solution. Goddard, whose own past includes a stint as a homicide detective in southern California and a writer of several published thriller novels, cautions anyone considering a crime against wildlife: "It used to be easy to get away with killing an animal. Well, things have changed. This laboratory can track you down years later. We can detect a little bit of blood on your clothing invisible to the naked eye and match it back to that killed animal with absolute statistical certainty."[32]

Catching up with poachers

One type of crime regularly targeted by the lab is poaching, or the killing of wildlife that is supposed to be safe from hunters. Poaching is a global problem, just as smuggling birds and other animals crosses international borders.

The lab used DNA to help solve a 1998 poaching case in Alaska when a hunter shot a mountain goat in Chugach State Park near Anchorage. He took the head to a taxidermist for mounting and left behind the bones and rotting carcass. The federal wildlife crime lab in Oregon compared DNA from the goat's head to DNA from the pile of rotting body parts left behind by the hunter. The DNA analysis confirmed that the head and the carcass came from the same animal, and the poacher was arrested.

DNA also helped game officials in Florida prosecute deer poachers. Ginger Clark, a senior biological scientist at the University of Florida, developed a technique that uses DNA to determine both the species and gender of an animal. This is especially important in Florida, where the hunting season for female deer lasts only two

days. Wildlife law enforcement officials in California also used DNA to prosecute deer poachers. After analyzing the DNA of deer meat in one man's freezer, game officials in California determined that his two hundred pounds of venison came from more individual deer than the hunting limit allowed.

The success of the lab at the University of Florida has motivated officials to seek its help in solving cases of illegal poaching of wild turkeys, alligators, turtles, and other

Indian authorities confiscated these white tiger skins. DNA evidence helps catch and stop poachers of protected species.

species. As a result of the work of this lab, game officials are now regularly equipped with DNA sampling kits to obtain genetic evidence out in the field.

In Canada, DNA technology has been used to target the problem of bear poaching. The DNA lab at the British Columbia Institute of Technology has created a database of bear DNA to keep tabs on the bear population and link poachers to their kill. Ernie Cooper, a wildlife enforcement officer with Environment Canada, explains how it works: "Let's suppose the carcass of a poached bear is found in the woods and a suspect is located who has bear meat in his freezer. Once this database is complete we will be able to use DNA matching to positively link that poached carcass to that suspect's bear meat and establish direct evidence to prosecute the offender."[33]

Since wild game hunters usually take some parts of their catch home and leave others where they fell, DNA now makes it possible for game wardens to match the body parts of animals that may be dispersed by miles. In Wyoming, a poacher was convicted of wanton destruction when six headless antelope carcasses were found near a city dump. DNA tests linked the carcasses to a buck antelope head that had been taken to a taxidermy shop for mounting. As Russ Pollard, a law enforcement coordinator for Wyoming Game and Fish explained: "We can now tie a blood spot or sample from an entrails pile to a head hanging in some guy's house or a steak in his freezer a year later."[34]

Do not believe everything you eat

There may be illegal bear meat in one man's freezer and too much venison in another's, but bear and deer at least do not masquerade as other forms of wildlife. DNA fingerprinting has revealed that restaurant patrons in New York and other large cities may be dining on delicacies they did not intend to order. A few years ago, scientists at the American Museum of Natural History in New York launched the so-called caviar project to determine the origin of caviar sold in that city.

Caviar is processed from fish eggs, or roe, spawned by sturgeon—large, bony, bottom feeders. Since each female sturgeon spawns only once every four years, the eggs are scarce, which adds to their value. There are many types of sturgeon, including black sturgeon, which produce some of the world's most prized caviar. Sturgeon roe can sell for up to several hundred dollars per pound, depending on the variety.

Researchers wanted to be certain that caviar connoisseurs in New York were actually getting their money's worth. They discovered that about 25 percent of the caviar sold in New York City was mislabeled. DNA proved that rather than having been spawned by Russian beluga sturgeon, as claimed on the labels, much of the caviar in New York was actually linked genetically to other fish, some of which are protected from commercial fishing.

DNA testing also uncovered another multimillion-dollar caviar scam in this country. U.S. Caviar & Caviar Ltd., a large American supplier of caviar, was convicted in 2000 of multiple violations of federal wildlife law. The company admitted importing tons of black market caviar from the United Arab Emirates and making it appear as if the caviar had been produced and exported by a legitimate Russian caviar supplier. It also exported some of the world's most expensive beluga and sevruga caviar from the Caspian Sea and deliberately mislabeled it so that it appeared to be a less expensive variety. In this way the company planned to avoid the more costly customs duties. DNA tests also revealed that some of the caviars the company claimed were the most costly and exotic varieties were actually the eggs of paddlefish and hackleback, fish native only to North America.

U.S. Caviar & Caviar Ltd. supplied many gourmet grocery chains and airlines with its products, whose fake labels were manufactured in the company's own Maryland headquarters. U.S. district judge Alexander Williams imposed a $10.4 million dollar fine on the company and three of its high-ranking officials. This was the largest fine ever imposed in a wildlife criminal case.

Sushi—oh no! I do not think so

Sushi, like caviar, is a delicacy that is vulnerable to fraud. It is not always easy to determine the exact ingredients in a sushi roll, as researchers from Harvard University discovered when they began making annual journeys to Japan's sushi markets. The *New York Times* reported that DNA revealed some unexpected ingredients to the scientists from Harvard's Center for Conservation and Evolutionary Genetics: "To their surprise, they found all sorts of things—dolphin, porpoise and even goat meat—being sold as highly expensive whale flesh at $50 to $100 a pound. About 30 percent of the whale for sale was from protected species."[35] Some whale meat is sold legally in Japan, but the sale of this delicacy is highly regulated, which adds to its value.

DNA analysis has been used to authenticate the ingredients used in such delicacies as caviar and sushi.

Three restaurants in Broward County, Florida, were also caught in sushi swindles. DNA tests verified that the restaurants were substituting sailfish, labeled falsely as tuna, in their sushi. Sailfish is a game fish that cannot be bought or sold under federal wildlife law. Captain Barry Cook of the Florida Fish and Wildlife Conservation Commission commented on the ability of DNA to pinpoint this kind of fraud, saying: "I wish I had had [DNA technology] years ago. This type of evidence is just that cut and dried."[36]

Whale and shark DNA

DNA fingerprinting may soon assume a large role in protecting animals that roam the sea from more than being rolled up into sushi. Many species of both shark and whale are at risk because their populations cannot keep up with the world's appetite for their meat. DNA helps scientists and organizations that protect wildlife keep track of the populations of these huge creatures in the world's oceans and focus worldwide attention on the issue of their declining numbers.

Worldwide demand for shark fin soup, an expensive Chinese delicacy, is one example of how entire populations of shark can be endangered by human tastes. In a brutal process called finning, fisherman catch 100 million sharks of many species each year and hack off their fins to make the soup, a bowl of which can cost up to $150. The animals are then dumped back into the sea without their fins to die a slow, painful death.

As a result of this practice, about fifty shark species are currently in danger. The population of the great white shark alone has decreased by 79 percent in the northwestern Atlantic Ocean. Scientist Mahmood Shivji at the Guy Harvey Research Institute of Nova Southeastern University in Florida developed a quick and inexpensive DNA fingerprint technique that can match a severed shark fin to a specific species of shark. Until the test was developed, it was almost impossible to link a severed fin to a shark species. Shivji's team is working to create a DNA database of all the shark species that are found in the world's fin markets so that their populations can be monitored.

DNA is also being used to track whale populations in the world's oceans. Whale hunting was banned by the International Whaling Commission (IWC) in 1986. But the moratorium on whale hunting is filled with special exceptions and exemptions, which makes the ban difficult to enforce. In South Korea, for example, whale meat can be sold legally if it was caught accidentally along the coast. In Japan, whale hunting is permitted only for research and not for food. A love for the taste of whale meat, however, contributes to a robust black market for this product in these countries, which officially support the whaling ban but unofficially allow an active trade in whale meat on the open market. Gina Lento, a scientist from New Zealand, and her colleagues made two trips a year to Japan and South Korea for four consecutive years in the late 1990s. They hired local investigators to pose as buyers in the fish markets. Using a portable laboratory, they tested the DNA in the meat samples. By comparing their samples to a whale DNA database, they could identify the types of whale meat being sold.

In one Japanese fish market the researchers found a piece of meat that could be traced to a humpback whale found only in Mexican waters. Lento commented on that discovery: "How can a Mexican whale turn up on a Japanese dinner plate? There is no evidence Mexican whales ever migrate into Japanese waters."[37] DNA also revealed Southern Hemisphere sei whale, Bryde's whale, North Pacific minke, fin whale, and blue whale for sale in Japanese markets. In another case, DNA fingerprinting helped trace meat that was being sold in two separate countries to the same whale, which was direct evidence of smuggling. Before the advent of DNA testing, it was almost impossible to distinguish one variety of whale meat from another, since all whale meat looks alike.

DNA has opened the window on what is actually happening in these countries. Earthtrust, a nonprofit organization dedicated to stemming the trade in illegal whale meat,

has actively employed DNA testing to further its goal. Its Saving Whales with DNA Project is a strategy for ending the global black market in whale meat through the use of DNA analysis. Earthtrust uses DNA to determine whether whale meat for sale is from a species that is allowed to be hunted or from one that is endangered. Earthtrust explains why DNA is used: "This is the single most powerful tool available to bring illegal trade to light and under control: even after an animal is killed and cut into tiny pieces, each piece can still tell the story of that animal's existence."[38] Earthtrust, like the IWC, has no enforcement power of its

A Hong Kong market sells shark fins for soup. DNA analysis allows conservationists to determine from which species a particular fin comes.

Japanese whalers cut their catch into pieces. DNA testing ensures that whale meat offered for sale comes from unprotected species.

own but depends on self-enforcement by individual countries. The hope is that international pressure will succeed in stemming the illegal export of whale products. For instance, in 2001, when DNA revealed that Norway was exporting minke whale products to Japan, Great Britain banned Norwegian whale research ships from its territorial waters.

In Australia, researchers at Southern Cross University are working to create a DNA database of individual humpback whales. They collect the DNA out in the open ocean from pieces of skin that have been shed by the whales as they breach or slap their tails and fins. The researchers lean over the front of their boat and scoop up the skin with an aquarium net attached to a pole. The goal is to track individual whales as they migrate around the world. Martin Elphinstone from Southern Cross explained how DNA will help researchers: "The point of the basic research is to generate this sort of database so that in future years someone can take a skin sample from South America or Tonga and say, 'Oh, that was a whale that was heading up the Great Barrier Reef three years ago.'"[39] By tracking individual whales, researchers will generate accurate records of

DNA data banks are being compiled in order to track the movements and population levels of endangered whale species like this humpback.

humpback populations. This information will help conservation groups and governments to protect these giant mammals, which, like many other whale species, have been hunted to the brink of extinction.

Using DNA to track a population of humpback whales highlights the major difference between the way DNA fingerprinting is used in wildlife law and human criminal justice. DNA is a tool of identification. In human law, DNA helps find the criminal. In wildlife law, DNA first identifies the crime. Wildlife law enforcement depends on DNA to identify the species of the victim, not just the identity of the criminal. DNA can reveal what species of bird or fish is developing inside a smuggled egg. DNA can tell investigators how many different deer have been killed and identify their gender. DNA can match a hunter's stuffed and mounted trophy to a leftover carcass thousands of miles away. DNA can expose the ingredients in a roll of sushi and unveil the true origin of a hunk of whale or a sliver of fin in a soup. This telltale genetic fingerprint has given a voice to wildlife that cannot speak out against its own exploitation. And DNA tells no false tales. By using DNA in this way, governments, scientists, and animal conservationists are gaining new strength in their battle to protect the animals that populate the earth.

5

DNA Evidence: Addressing the Issues

IT HAS BEEN less than two decades since DNA was used for the first time to solve a murder. Since then, scientists, the police, those who prosecute crime, and those who defend the accused have found ways to use the twists and turns of this molecule to further their causes. DNA, the molecule that nestles within most cells, has become firmly implanted as a tool of the criminal justice system. Despite its widespread use and its many successes, there are still issues that surround its use. Lawmakers wrestle with how to reconcile the rights of the individual as guaranteed in the Constitution with the welfare of the public as a whole. Other issues concern the practical problems that arise when a new technology such as DNA fingerprinting is in such demand that it becomes nearly impossible to oversee and control all the factors that affect it. Court decisions, debates, and new laws enacted by state and federal legislatures all reflect a society in the process of grappling with these difficult questions. It is an ongoing process.

Whose DNA should be deposited in the data bank?

Ever since Virginia passed the first state law in 1989 requiring certain offenders to submit DNA samples for a permanent state DNA data bank, questions have been raised nationwide about whose DNA should be stored in data banks, for how long, and who should have access to this information. DNA, unlike a standard fingerprint, is more than a simple means of identification. DNA contains all the genetic information about an individual. Biological family history and even certain physical and mental diseases are all contained in an individual's unique genetic code. In this country, personal information such as this is considered private. Storing that much private information in the public records is worrisome to many who fear that the information could be easily misused. In his book *Signs of Life*, Robert Pollack explains how access to DNA information compromises personal privacy: "The latent risk of loss of privacy is growing rapidly; keeping and analyzing people's DNA without specific, agreed upon legal authority is like reading their mail or tapping their phones without a warrant."[40] Many others fear that DNA information could be used to deny employment or health insurance to individuals considered at risk for certain diseases.

But others believe that it is possible both to regulate access to DNA data banks and guard the safety of every community by collecting DNA not just from criminals, but from every individual born in this country. This topic was addressed by the National Commission on the Future of DNA Evidence that was formed by Attorney General Janet Reno during the Clinton administration. The purpose of the commission was to provide the attorney general with recommendations on the use of DNA from the crime scene to the courtroom. Michael E. Smith, a University of Wisconsin law professor who participated in the commission, believes that a universal data bank would help prevent crime. He said that such a data bank "would make DNA a true deterrent to crime, which it cannot be so long as the DNA databanks contain only information on known criminals and suspects."[41] His opinion has been echoed by many others, including James Watson, one of the scientists who discovered the double-helix shape of this molecule over fifty years ago. New York's former mayor Rudolph Giuliani once suggested taking DNA from every newborn in this country and storing it indefinitely for the purpose of criminal identification.

An analyst checks a sample of blood at a DNA data bank. Some people believe that every individual should be required to submit DNA samples to such banks.

While collecting the DNA of every newborn may happen sometime in the future, collecting the DNA of juveniles who have committed crimes is a present source of controversy. In the past century, a juvenile justice system has developed in this country that treats young offenders differently from their adult counterparts. This has been based on the notion that if a young person commits a crime, there is hope that he or she will still grow up to lead a productive, law-abiding life. To aid youthful offenders in this way, it has been customary to seal or even expunge their criminal records after a certain period of time to protect them from being permanently affected by mistakes made when they were young. Sealed criminal records cannot be used to deny employment or college admission or even as evidence of prior criminal history. However, by

1999, when thirty states had expanded their data banking laws to include juveniles, not one of those states required that DNA records be sealed when the juveniles became legal adults. In fact, Arizona expressly prohibits expunging juvenile DNA records. Texas law goes even further by giving the state's youth commission the duty of overseeing juvenile fingerprints and arrest records and directing that juvenile DNA information be entered into the adult data bank.

Some lawmakers believe that the practice of maintaining juvenile DNA records is justified by the realistic expectation that today's juvenile offender will become tomorrow's adult criminal. Jonathan Kimmelman dis-

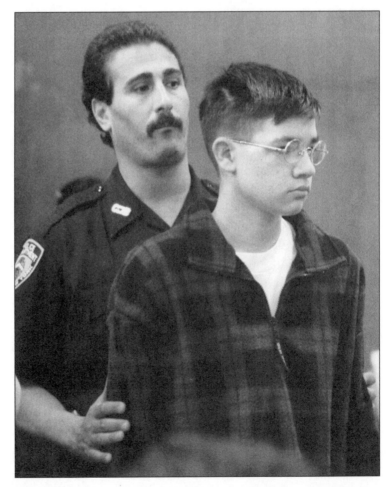

In many states, juvenile offenders must submit DNA for a data bank. Critics fear that such DNA records could make juvenile offenders lifelong suspects.

cussed this debate in an issue of the *Journal of Law, Medicine, and Ethics* when he wrote: "This practice undermines a juvenile justice system that has been about the ideal of rehabilitation. In effect, juvenile offenders become suspects for life when their profiles are permanently entered into databanks, which is inconsistent with the historical practice of expunging juvenile crime records."[42] The federal government also supports the collection and preservation of the DNA of juvenile offenders. In April 2003, *USA Today* reported that the Bush administration proposed adding juvenile DNA profiles to the FBI's national database, CODIS.

DNA and the Constitution

Along with issues about whose DNA to bank and how long to keep those records, DNA data banks have also raised Constitutional issues. The Fourth Amendment protects citizens from unreasonable search and seizure. That means anyone from the government, including the police, must have specific permission to search or take private property. That permission comes in the form of a search warrant that is issued by a judge. Before a judge will issue a search warrant, the police must have enough evidence—called probable cause—that a suspect committed a specific crime. DNA testing is considered a form of search, and so the same probable cause is necessary before a person can be required by the police to supply a DNA sample. Many believe that the same standard of probable cause should be required before law enforcement officials are permitted to conduct random searches of DNA data banks. Decisions about data bank searches could have far-reaching effects on some standard practices in law enforcement. Data bank searches are regularly conducted by police hoping to revive cold cases. The increasing use of John Doe warrants to extend the statutes of limitations on specific crimes also depends on random data bank searches to link genetic profiles with the names of specific criminals.

So far, only one federal court has issued a decision about the constitutionality of data bank searches. In October

2003, a three-judge panel of the Ninth U.S. Circuit Court of Appeals ruled that requiring blood samples from inmates and convicts on parole for the FBI DNA database was unconstitutional. In his decision, Judge Stephen Reinhardt wrote that the blood samples "violate the Fourth Amendment protection against illegal searches because they constitute suspicionless searches with the objective of furthering law enforcement purposes."[43] The ruling was based on the fact that DNA information can be searched randomly without legal suspicion that a former convict has been involved in a specific crime. It is still not clear how that ruling will affect many cold cases that were solved with searches of the federal DNA data banks.

Genetic dragnets and DNA evidence

Another controversy raised by collecting large numbers of genetic profiles to find one suspect is the very concept of the genetic dragnet itself. When DNA was used to solve the Narborough murders in 1987, police requested that every male in three neighboring villages voluntarily submit his DNA for testing. Since then, this type of mass DNA screening has become more common. Recently, police asked eight hundred men in southern Louisiana for permission to swab the insides of their mouths for DNA in a search for a serial rapist. The *New York Times* reported what happened when one man, Shannon Kohler, voiced his reluctance to participate in the voluntary effort to screen his DNA: "It was his choice, Mr. Kohler said the officers told him, but if he refused, they would get a court order and that would get in the newspapers and then everyone would know he was not cooperating."[44] Kohler, a forty-four-year-old welder, insisted that his Constitutional rights had been violated by both the pressure to submit his DNA and the placement of his DNA in the citywide DNA database. He said: "These rights are what make America America to me."[45]

Some critics of genetic dragnets believe that these dragnets also violate the Fifth Amendment to the Constitution, which protects individuals from being forced to testify

against themselves. So far, however, these objections have not resulted in court rulings that outlaw DNA dragnets. In Massachusetts in 1999, DNA testing of 32 men who lived or worked at a nursing home where a resident had been impregnated resulted in the successful prosecution of a nurse's aide. In Los Angeles that same year, detectives reopened a fourteen-year-old case in which a sheriff's deputy had been killed. As they were testing the 165 potential suspects, 1 suspect whose DNA matched the evidence committed suicide before he could be arrested.

The same Constitutional objections have been raised to the surreptitious methods frequently used by the police to collect DNA evidence. If a search warrant and probable cause are required before a suspect can be compelled to submit to a DNA test, then many believe that the same legal level of suspicion must be demonstrated before any DNA evidence is collected. Civil libertarians are troubled by the Constitutional issues raised by taking DNA from

A police officer collects saliva from a man during a mass DNA screening. Some argue that such dragnets violate the provisions of the Fifth Amendment.

cigarette butts discarded on the sidewalk or envelopes innocently licked by possible suspects. So far, the courts have not specifically ruled against these practices, but legal scholars wrestle with these unclear boundaries between an individual's right to privacy and the safety of the public.

Problems with police procedure

While interpreting the Constitution is complex, the process of collecting DNA from a crime scene and making sure that it is handled properly seems straightforward. But so far, national standards and quality controls have been inconsistent. The possibility of contamination, the inability to account for the whereabouts of DNA evidence, and questions about police procedures have all contributed to the loss of court cases involving DNA.

Questions about procedures followed by the Los Angeles Police Department were crucial in the defense of Orenthal James (O.J.) Simpson, the former football star who was accused of murdering his ex-wife Nicole Brown Simpson and her friend Ronald Goldman in 1994. The murder occurred one summer evening in an affluent neighborhood in Los Angeles. DNA was a major player in the attempt of the prosecution to pin guilt for these gruesome crimes on the former star running back for the Buffalo Bills. During the trial, prosecutors, defense attorneys, forensic experts, and others spent two months arguing over forty-five blood samples that had been taken from Simpson's house on Rockingham Avenue, his white Bronco, and his socks. The evidence seemed convincing. Dominick Dunne, a writer who covered the trial for *Vanity Fair* magazine, described the prosecution's key testimony:

> Along came Dr. Robin Cotton, director of laboratories for Cellmark Diagnostics, the nation's largest private forensic DNA-testing firm, to present the trial's defining moment. Dr. Cotton, who holds a Ph.D. in molecular biology and biochemistry from the University of California, Irvine, explained the basics of DNA to the jurors in a prim, precise manner, as a favorite schoolteacher might, simplifying the complicated material but never talking down to them. According to Cotton, the blood found near the victims could have come from only

Bloodstained sheets were part of the seemingly irrefutable evidence submitted by the prosecution in the O.J. Simpson murder trial.

1 person in 170 million African-Americans or Caucasians. That blood matched O.J. Simpson's blood. The blood on the sock in Simpson's bedroom was consistent with that of only 1 person out of 6.8 billion—more people than there are on earth—and that blood matched the blood of Nicole Brown Simpson.[46]

Despite the seeming irrefutability of these numbers, doubt was raised when the defense argued that police detectives on the case were sloppy and imprecise in their evidence collection procedures. One of the collection vials was missing 1.5 milliliters of blood, and some blood evidence discovered by the police contained a preservative. In addition, the police could not account for where some of

Forensic expert Henry Lee testified in the Simpson trial that authorities had mishandled the blood samples submitted as evidence.

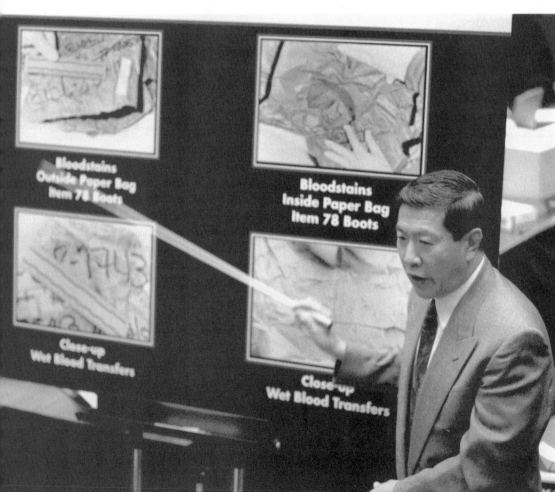

the blood had been stored for part of the time, meaning the chain of custody had been broken. The defense used these flaws in police procedure to suggest that evidence had been planted by the police in their zeal to prosecute Simpson. To convince the jurors that the DNA results could not be trusted in this case, the defense called Dr. Henry Lee as a witness. Lee is considered one of the foremost forensic scientists in the world. He is chief of the Connecticut State Police Forensic Science Laboratory and has investigated over six thousand homicide cases. Lee testified that the police ignored some blood spots, contaminated others, and stored blood samples improperly. Lee's testimony was crucial to the defense's case. When all the testimony ended, the jury ruled that the prosecution had not satisfied its burden of proof. Simpson was acquitted of both murders.

Most legal experts agree that one of the most important lessons learned from the Simpson trial was the importance of establishing formal and consistent procedures for collecting and preserving DNA evidence. Law enforcement agencies all over the country recognize the need for formalizing evidence collection procedures. But only a small number of jurisdictions has made this a priority. In San Diego, the detective assigned to a case works with lab personnel to determine exactly which evidence will be analyzed. Deputies in the San Diego Sheriff's Department are carefully trained in DNA collection procedures. An article in the *San Diego Union Tribune* explains why:

> In the new world of forensic science, the training of front-line law enforcement becomes a new priority, the quality of the evidence being only as good as the skill of those who identify it and collect it. Sheriff's detectives long ago earned a reputation for being on top of their game in this arena and now the department has committed itself to creating an unbroken chain of expertise: from the deputy on the street to the investigator on the case through the forensic laboratory and into the courtroom.[47]

Many other cities are in the process of establishing formal evidence-collecting procedures, but national standards have not yet been established.

Training of lab technicians

Another problem that has become evident is that many lab technicians have been inadequately trained to handle and analyze DNA evidence. Since there are no consistent standards for training DNA lab technicians, different labs require different levels of training. Stephen B. Bright, the director of the Southern Center for Human Rights, commented on the inadequate training of many lab technicians: "So many of the people who give DNA testimony went to two weeks of training by the F.B.I. in Quantico [Virginia], say, and they are miraculously transformed from beat policemen into forensic scientists."[48] There have been several cases in which inadequate training has resulted in miscarriages of justice. In Arizona, for example, defendants and their attorneys in nine criminal cases were notified in 2003 that the Phoenix Police Crime Lab had made errors analyzing DNA evidence in six homicides, two rapes, and an aggravated assault.

One of the most serious examples of poor crime lab work was uncovered at the police crime lab in Houston, Texas, in 2003. Josiah Sutton was one victim of this lab. He was only sixteen in 1998 when his DNA was tested and reported to match DNA found on a rape victim. He was convicted and sent to prison for twenty-five years. New testing in 2003 not only exonerated Sutton, but also condemned the crime lab that had conducted the DNA tests. An audit of 525 of its case files involving DNA testing uncovered so many errors that the lab's operation was suspended in 2003. The *New York Times* reported on the problems: "The audit of the Houston laboratory found that technicians had misinterpreted data, were poorly trained and kept shoddy records. In most cases, they used up all available evidence, barring defense experts from refuting or verifying their results. Even the laboratory's building was a mess, with a leaky roof having contaminated evidence."[49] The analyst who testified in Sutton's case had attended only a two-week training course sponsored by the company that sold DNA kits to the lab.

The discovery that many local labs have problems has led to a broad investigation of the practices of the national

FBI lab, since many of its DNA fingerprints originate at local police crime labs. A forensic technician from the FBI's own lab was also found to have ignored required procedures for two years.

To help ensure that crime labs responsible for analyzing DNA evidence are run according to the strictest standards, they can become accredited by the American Society of Crime Lab Directors (ASCLD). This voluntary process requires labs to follow strict guidelines for training, procedures, cleanliness, safety, and security. A team of forensic experts spends months overseeing a lab's operations before

Josiah Sutton (right) was released from prison in 2003 when retesting of DNA samples exonerated him of rape charges.

granting its seal of approval. Nearly 250 local, state, federal, and private crime labs in thirty-seven states, the District of Columbia, and five foreign countries have been accredited by ASCLD. Meanwhile, thousands of other labs lacking accreditation still have the responsibility for analyzing evidence and making determinations in criminal cases.

Lab funding and growing evidence backlogs

Even when lab technicians have adequate training, many crime labs are so overloaded with cases that the quality of their work suffers. Each DNA analyst in Houston had 40 to 60 cases a month. Typically, analysts are expected to handle 60 to 120 cases a year in most cities, according to Arthur Eisenberg, director of the DNA Identity Laboratory at the University of North Texas Health Science Center. Eisenberg helped establish FBI standards for DNA labs. "To have two analysts for a city the size of Houston in itself is criminal,"[50] he said. The fact that many lab technicians are overloaded means there is a growing backlog of cases awaiting DNA testing. The states have a combined backlog of 350,000 untested DNA samples for rapes and homicides alone. In addition, about 300,000 more DNA samples taken from convicted offenders still await screening.

In 2003, the Bush administration announced plans to commit $1 billion within a five-year period to help eliminate this backlog. The plan was announced by Attorney General John Ashcroft, who explained that the plan includes funds for testing the DNA of convicted felons who claim to be innocent. Ashcroft said that the plan would also expand the types of crimes included in the national DNA database so that the DNA of all people convicted of violence or terrorism would become part of the database. When the plan is in operation, states that currently collect DNA from people who are arrested but never convicted will be permitted to enter those genetic fingerprints into the national database.

Many advocates for convicted offenders criticize the Bush plan for not providing enough funds for postconviction testing. Lawrence Goldman, president of the National Association of Criminal Defense Lawyers, said that the administration's proposal to provide the states with $5 million is insufficient: "I would have preferred that more than a pittance be given to post-conviction testing. There are people languishing in jails for years and years."[51] Others, such as Innocence Project codirector Peter Neufeld, question the motives of the Bush administration. Neufeld believes the plan gives too much power to the Justice Department to decide who should have access to DNA testing. Neufeld and others are concerned that the administration is limiting the funds for postconviction testing while it broadens the categories of offenders and suspects whose DNA fingerprints are permanently entered in the federal database.

Funding for most crime labs, however, still comes primarily from the individual states. Tight state budgets make it difficult to fund the labs sufficiently to catch up with the constantly growing backlogs of DNA samples. In an editorial in January 2004, the *Detroit News* called on the Michigan State Parole Board to alter its policies so that less risky inmates are released. The money saved by the state on their incarceration could then be applied to crime lab funding. The editorial also suggested that ill and elderly prisoners should be released for the same reason. Michigan currently supports three crime labs capable of DNA testing. Each lab costs the state $7.3 million per year. Other states are finding unique ways to fund their labs. A state DNA missing persons lab in California is funded through a $2 fee on death certificates. After two years of assessing that fee, enough money was raised to pay for an analyst, a supervisor, an administrator, and a technician.

DNA testing with its pinpoint accuracy has changed criminal science forever. But this exquisite accuracy also carries responsibility. Mistakes become less acceptable as the means for preventing them become available. Those who wrote the Constitution of the United States could not have imagined that the ideals that guided them, such as justice and individual privacy, would one day be both challenged

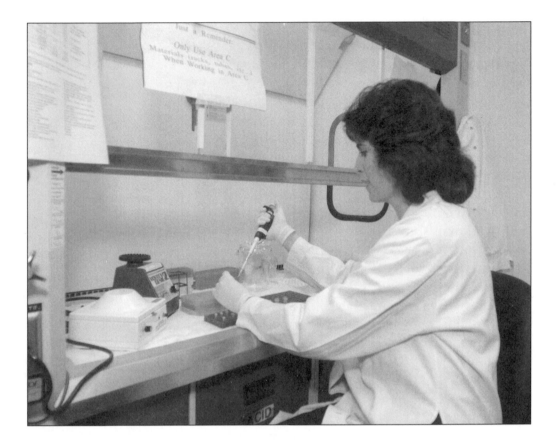

Despite the problems involved with collecting and storing DNA evidence, DNA testing remains a very effective criminal-science tool.

and supported by a tiny molecule. This molecule has uncovered more than new evidence. It has also made it clear that there are still decisions that need to be made: decisions about DNA lab funding, evidence collection procedures, data banking, and training of technicians. These decisions must be guided not by a search for guilt or innocence but by a search for justice. Dr. Henry Lee agrees. He says in his book *Cracking Cases:* "Our entire American system of jurisprudence is grounded in the concept of equal protection and fair play for all. We can demand no less, no matter where the trail of forensic evidence takes us."[52] It is important that those who make the policies and those who follow them are guided by the original intentions of the Constitution—to promote and protect the welfare of all.

Notes

Chapter 1: A Powerful New Crime-Solving Tool

1. Barry Scheck, Peter Neufeld, and Jim Dwyer, *Actual Innocence*. New York: Signet, p. 2001, xx.

2. Quoted in Joseph Wambaugh, *The Blooding*. New York: William Morrow, 1989, p. 80.

3. James Watson, *DNA: The Secret of Life*. New York: Knopf, 2003, p. xi.

4. Quoted in Wambaugh, *The Blooding*, pp. 81–82.

5. Scheck et al., *Actual Innocence*, p. 46.

6. Watson, *DNA*, p. 270.

7. Quoted in Georgia Bureau of Investigation, Division of Forensic Scientists, Trace Evidence Section, www.ganet.org/gbi/trace_evidence.html.

Chapter 2: Convicting the Guilty

8. Quoted in Harlan Levy, *And the Blood Cried Out*. New York: Basic Books, 1996, p. 96.

9. Levy, *And the Blood Cried Out*, p. 101.

10. *San Diego Union Tribune*, "Slain Cockatoo Stars as Witness in Trial," February 19, 2003, p. A7.

11. Quoted in CBSNews.com, "DNA Solves Crimes Too," March 29, 2001. www.cbsnews.com/stories/2001/03/29/eveningnews/printable282554.shtml.

12. Levy, *And the Blood Cried Out*, p. 150.

13. Quoted in Judy Muller, "Old Crimes Solved with New Technology," ABC News, May 10, 2003. www.abcnews.com.

14. Quoted in David M. Halbfinger, "Police Dragnets for

DNA Tests Draw Criticism," *New York Times*, January 1, 2003, p. 41.

15. Quoted in Watson, *DNA*, p. 276.

16. Quoted in William K. Rashbaum, "New York Pursues Old Cases of Rape Based Just on DNA," *New York Times*, August 5, 2003, p. A1.

Chapter 3: Freeing the Innocent

17. Quoted in Eric Berger, "DNA Analysis Becoming More Precise, Pervasive," *Houston Chronicle*, March 16, 2003. www.HoustonChronicle.com.

18. Scheck et al., *Actual Innocence*, p. 157.

19. National Public Radio, *This American Life*, May 24, 2003.

20. Scheck et al., *Actual Innocence*, p. 286.

21. Scheck et al., *Actual Innocence*, p. xviii.

22. Innocence Project, home page, www.innocenceproject. org.

23. Quoted in Associated Press, "Spread of Innocence Projects Seen as New Civil Rights Movement," *Dallas Morning News*, June 6, 2002. www.DallasNews.com.

24. Quoted in Associated Press, "Spread of Innocence Projects Seen as New Civil Rights Movement."

25. Quoted in United Press International, "Commentary Faceoff: To Test or Not to Test," ClariNet, September 29, 2003. http://quickstart.clari.net/qs_se/webnews/wed/cx/Uface off-dna.Rlul_DST.html.

26. Quoted in Associated Press, "Prisoners Face Deadline to Ask for DNA Testing," *San Diego Union Tribune*, September 26, 2003, p. A15.

27. Quoted in Innocence Project, "DNA News." www.inno-cenceproject.org/dnanews/index.php.

28. Quoted in Pam Belluck, "Push in Massacusetts for a

Death Penalty," *New York Times*, September 22, 2003. www. nytimes.com

29. Quoted in Frank Phillips, "Science Stressed in Death Penalty," *Boston Globe*, September 24, 2003. www.Boston. com.

Chapter 4: Protecting Wildlife

30. Quoted in Quantum ABC TV, "Egg Smuggler," March 8, 2001. www.abc.net.au/quantum/S253003.htm.

31. Quoted in Arctic Science Journeys, "DNA Detectives," www.uaf.edu/seagrant/NewsMedia/98ASJ/04.16.98_DNA. html.

32. Quoted in Michelle Pahl, "U.S. Animal Detectives Fight Crime in Forensics Lab," *National Geographic Today*, April 2, 2003. http://nationalgeographic.com/news/2003.

33. Quoted in British Columbia Institute of Technology, "Poachers Beware: New DNA Forensics Helps Nab Illegal Wildlife Traders," news release, December 19, 2000. www. newsreleases.bcit.ca/200012/forensics-bear-dna.shtml.

34. Quoted in Mindy Sink, "Genetic Pawprints Are Leading Game Wardens to Poachers," *New York Times*, May 26, 1998, sec. F, p. 4.

35. Alexander Stille, "New Mission for DNA: Preservation," *New York Times*, February 12, 2000, sec. B, p. 9.

36. Quoted in Environmental News Network, "DNA Technology Busts Wildlife Poachers," CNN.com, May 29, 2000. www.cnn.com/nature.

37. Quoted in Ray Lilley, "Evidence of Illegal Whale Trade Uncovered in New Zealand," Environmental Media Services, May 12, 1998. www.ems.org/whales/endangered-whales-trade.html.

38. Earthtrust, "Saving Whales with DNA." www.earth-trust.org/dnaproj.html.

39. Quoted in The Science Show, "Whale DNA," December 16, 2000. www.abc.net.au/rn/science/ss/stories/s223982. htm.

Chapter 5: DNA Evidence: Addressing the Issues

40. Robert Pollack, *Signs of Life: The Language and Meaning of DNA*. Boston: Houghton Mifflin, 1994, p. 109.

41. Quoted in Halbfinger, "Police Dragnets for DNA Tests Draw Criticism," p. 41.

42. Jonathan Kimmelman, "Risking Ethical Insolvency: A Survey of Trends on Criminal DNA Databanking," *Journal of Law, Medicine, Ethics*, Fall 2000. www.aslme.org/pub_jlme/28.3h.php.

43. David Kravets, "Law Requiring Blood Samples from U.S. Convicts Is Voided," *San Diego Union Tribune*, Friday, October 3, 2003, p. A3.

44. Halbfinger, "Police Dragnets for DNA Tests Draw Criticism," p. 41.

45. Quoted in Halbfinger, "Police Dragnets for DNA Tests Draw Criticism," p. 41.

46. Dominick Dunne, *Justice: Crimes, Trials, and Punishments*. New York: Crown Publishers, 2001, p. 182.

47. Greg Thompson and Emily Williams, "The Thin Blue Line's New Front Line," *San Diego Union Tribune*, July 27, 2003, p. G1.

48. Quoted in Adam Liptak, "You Think DNA Evidence Is Foolproof? Try Again," *New York Times*, March 16, 2003, p. 5.

49. Adam Liptak, "Review of DNA from Houston Police Crime Lab Clears Man Convicted of Rape," *New York Times*, March 11, 2003, p. A12.

50. Quoted in Pam Easton, "Houston Re-examines DNA Lab's Results," *San Diego Union Tribune*, March 24, 2003, p. A12.

51. Quoted in Eric Lichtblau, "Bush Plan Expands DNA Tests in Crimes," *San Diego Union Tribune*, March 12, 2003, p. A8.

52. Henry Lee, *Cracking Cases: The Science of Solving Crimes*. New York: Prometheus Books, 2002, p. 229.

Organizations
to Contact

The American Civil Liberties Union (ACLU)

125 Broad St., 18th Floor, New York, NY 10004-2400
(212) 549-2500
(212) 549-2646
www.aclu.org

The ACLU is a nonprofit watchdog organization dedicated to protecting the civil liberties of individuals and communities from government abuse. It has many causes, including opposition to the death penalty, protection from government surveillance, and making sure that personal information remains private and is not used against individuals by the government.

The Innocence Project

Benjamin N. Cardozo School of Law
100 5th Ave.
3rd Floor
New York, NY 10003
www.innocenceproject.org

Created in 1992 by Barry Scheck and Peter Neufeld, this nonprofit legal clinic handles cases in which postconviction DNA testing can yield conclusive proof of innocence. There are many other Innocence Projects around the country, including the California Innocence Project based at the California Western School of Law.

U.S. Fish and Wildlife Service (FWS)

U.S. Department of the Interior
1849 C St. NW

Washington, DC 20240
(202) 208-3100
www.fws.gov

The U.S. Fish and Wildlife Service is a government agency that oversees regional offices, national wildlife refuges, and research and development centers whose purpose is to conserve and protect endangered species and their habitats. The National Fish and Wildlife Forensics Laboratory in Ashland, Oregon, is part of the FWS.

For Further Reading

Books

Helen Cothran, ed., *Endangered Species.* San Diego: Greenhaven Press, 2001. One of the books in the Opposing Viewpoints series, this collection contains passionate opinions on both sides of many issues related to the protection of wildlife and how to balance the needs of wildlife with the needs of society.

Ron Fridell, *Solving Crimes: Pioneers of Forensic Science.* New York: Franklin Watts, 2000. This book covers the roles of six men over the past century in advancing the role that forensics plays in solving crimes. Includes a discussion of Alec Jeffreys's development of genetic fingerprinting.

Leon Friedman, *The Supreme Court.* New York: Chelsea House, 1987. An introduction to the "greatest court in the land," this book explains the Supreme Court's history and development as well as how it functions to guard individual freedoms. Good description of how the Supreme Court works to protect the powers of the states and interpret the Constitution.

N.E. Genge, *The Forensic Casebook: The Science of Crime Scene Investigation.* New York: Ballantine Books, 2002. A complete and informative encyclopedia of forensic evidence and how it is evaluated.

Joel Herskowitz, *Double Talking Helix Blues.* New York: Cold Spring Harbor Laboratory Press, 1993. Illustrations by Judy Cuddihy and a cassette-tape recording of this talking blues song make this picture-book-style text fun to follow and informative to hear. Describes the basic function of DNA.

Charlotte Foltz Jones, *Fingerprints and Talking Bones: How Real Life Crimes Are Solved.* New York: Delacorte Press, 1997. This book contains many examples of various types of evidence and how they are used to solve crimes. It also includes chapters on clues from the body, bugs, cars, and animals, and it has a good explanation of DNA fingerprinting.

Christopher Lampton, *DNA Fingerprinting.* New York: Franklin Watts, 1991. This book examines procedures and uses of DNA as a method of identification in criminal science.

Milton Meltzer, *Case Closed: The Real Scoop on Detective Work.* New York: Orchard Books, 2001. A close examination of the history, changing technologies, and challenges of detective work.

Mary Williams, ed., *The Death Penalty.* San Diego: Greenhaven Press, 2002. Part of the Opposing Viewpoints series, this book demonstrates that as early as the 1700s, arguments raged about the death penalty: whether it deters crime, whether it is just, and whether it violates the Constitution's protections against cruel and unusual punishment. Includes a discussion of how DNA is changing the debate.

Web Sites

American Museum of Natural History
(http://ology.amnh.org/genetics/index.html). Activities, games, projects, and interesting facts about genetics are presented in a user-friendly format. The resources of the Museum of Natural History are extensive and used to make this topic accessible for all ages.

Death Penalty Information
(www.deathpenaltyinfo.msu.edu). "Death Penalty Information for High School" was designed principally by the Michigan State Communication Technology Laboratory with input from the Death Penalty Information Center. This

easy-to-navigate site includes sections about the history of the death penalty, with arguments presented by both proponents and opponents, and discussions of the ethics and justice surrounding capital punishment.

The Federal Bureau of Investigation (www.fbi.gov). Follow the "For the Family" link to the FBI page for kids in grades six to twelve to participate in an FBI case from start to finish. Links explain each part of the process in more detail, including one that connects the reader to the DNA Analysis unit.

How Stuff Works (http://science.howstuffworks.com/dna-evidence). The article "How DNA Evidence Works" by Ann Meeker O'Connell uses real photos of DNA fingerprints to make this site interesting and informative. A table of contents provides several options for more information.

Newspapers in Education
(www.cincinnati.com/nie/archive/08-28-01). For grade levels nine to twelve, this site begins with an explanation of how DNA evidence freed a man who spent seventeen years on death row for the 1982 murder of a nine-year-old girl. It is followed by a lesson about DNA testing and its applications in modern forensic criminology, with links to other information about DNA.

Works Consulted

Books

Michael Baden and Marion Roach, *Dead Reckoning: The New Science of Catching Killers.* New York: Simon & Schuster, 2001. This book discusses the science involved in criminal investigation, from autopsies to the science of bugs. Baden was chief forensic pathologist for the investigations into the deaths of John F. Kennedy and Martin Luther King. The mistakes made in the O.J. Simpson trial are discussed.

Ethan Bier, *The Coiled Spring.* New York: Cold Spring Harbor Laboratory Press, 2000. Geneticist Ethan Bier presents the science of genetics in detail for both experts and budding scientists. Written for college students, his text uses many metaphors to help clarify the complex science involved.

Joseph Bosco, *A Problem of Evidence: How the Prosecution Freed O.J. Simpson.* New York, William Morrow, 1996. Written by a crime journalist, this book describes how the prosecution bungled the case against O.J. Simpson.

Dominick Dunne, *Justice: Crimes, Trials, and Punishments.* New York: Crown Publishers, 2001. A collection of stories about cases and trials that Dunne covered for *Vanity Fair* magazine. He began his writing career writing about the very personal murder of his own daughter, Dominique.

Henry Lee, *Cracking Cases: The Science of Solving Crimes.* New York: Prometheus Books, 2002. Written by one of the foremost forensic scientists in the world, this is a fascinating account of five of the most famous cases of modern times, including the trial of O.J. Simpson.

Harlan Levy, *And the Blood Cried Out.* New York: Basic Books, 1996. A prosecutor's account of how DNA and other forensic evidence has furthered the goals of the criminal justice system. Levy shows how many important cases have hinged on DNA evidence, including the World Trade Center bombing in 1993, the O.J. Simpson case, and the case against the Central Park jogger. He also explores the power and problems of DNA evidence.

Brian Marriner, On *Death's Bloody Trail: Murder and the Art of Forensic Science.* New York: St. Martin's, 1993. A behind-the-scenes look at the actual methods used by investigators to put killers behind bars. Uses case histories to illustrate how forensic science has developed over the last century.

Robert Pollack, *Signs of Life: The Language and Meaning of DNA.* Boston: Houghton Mifflin, 1994. Pollack is a molecular geneticist. He explains DNA as a metaphor for a work of literature and shows how it can be read and understood in different ways. He also discusses the responsibility that he feels goes along with man's ability to use DNA.

Barry Scheck, Peter Neufeld, and Jim Dwyer, *Actual Innocence.* New York: Signet, 2001. Written by the founders of the Innocence Project at the Benjamin N. Cardozo School of Law, this is an account of how DNA functions as a tool and how it has highlighted mistakes and injustices within the criminal justice system

Joseph Wambaugh, *The Blooding.* New York: William Morrow, 1989. Wambaugh, a former policeman, wrote this account of the Narborough murders, their investigation, and the way the case was finally solved.

James Watson, *DNA: The Secret of Life.* New York: Knopf, 2003. This book was written by one of the scientists who received the Nobel Prize for the discovery of the structure of DNA. Published in the year that marked the fiftieth anniversary of that discovery, this book covers all the roles played by this significant molecule, including its role in the criminal justice system.

Jon Zonderman, *Beyond the Crime Lab: The New Science of Investigation*. New York: Wiley, 1999. This book contains a complete discussion of forensic science, including how physical evidence is analyzed and the techniques used in the crime lab. It also explores issues of forensics and civil liberties.

Periodicals

Associated Press, "Prisoners Face Deadline to Ask for DNA Testing," *San Diego Union Tribune*, September 26, 2003.

Justin Brooks, "How Many More Innocent People Sit in Prison?" *San Diego Union Tribune*, January 16, 2003.

Dallas Morning News, "Spread of Innocence Projects Seen as New Civil Rights Movement," June 6, 2002.

James Dao, "In Same Case, DNA Clears Convict and Finds Suspect," *New York Times*, September 6, 2003.

Edwin Dobb, "False Confessions," *Amnesty Now*, Winter 2002.

Jim Dwyer, "Likely U-Turn by Prosecutors in 1989 Attack," *New York Times*, October 12, 1989.

Jim Dwyer and Kevin Flynn, "New Light on Jogger's Rape Calls Evidence into Question," *New York Times*, December 1, 2002.

———, "Prosecutor Is Said to Back Dismissals in '89 Jogger Rape," *New York Times*, December 5, 2002.

Pam Easton, "Houston Re-exammes DNA Lab's Results," *San Diego Union Tribune*, March 24, 2003.

Elissa Gootman, "DNA Evidence Helps Three Men Gain Release in 1985 Murder Convictions," *New York Times*, June 12, 2003.

David M. Halbfinger, "Police Dragnets for DNA Tests Draw Criticism," *New York Times*, January 1, 2003.

Erin Hallissy, "State's DNA Lab Has Scored Series of Early Successes," *San Francisco Chronicle*, April 19, 2003.

J. Harry Jones, "Death Penalty Focus of Erskine Case," *San Diego Union Tribune*, September 22, 2003.

David Kravets, "Law Requiring Blood Samples from U.S. Convicts Is Voided," *San Diego Union Tribune*, October 3, 2003.

Karen Young Kreeger, "Dramatic Growth in DNA-Based Forensics Doesn't Translate into Job Opportunities," *Scientist*, April 17, 1995.

Dune Lawrence, "Exhibit Aims to Simplify How Human Genome Works," *San Diego Union Tribune*, June 7, 2003.

Eric Lichtblau, "Bush Plan Expands DNA Tests in Crimes," *San Diego Union Tribune*, March 12, 2003.

Adam Liptak, "Death Row Numbers Decline as Challenges to System Rise," *New York Times*, January 11, 2003.

———, "Prosecutors Fight DNA Use for Exoneration," *New York Times*, August 29, 2003.

———, "Review of DNA from Houston Police Crime Lab Clears Man Convicted of Rape," *New York Times*, March 11, 2003.

———, "You Think DNA Evidence Is Foolproof? Try Again," *New York Times*, March 16, 2003.

Laura Mansnerus, "States Seek Ways to Make Executions Error Free," *New York Times*, November 2, 2003.

Bret Martel, "Fate of DNA Samples Taken in Serial Killer Case Becomes an Issue," May 31, 2003.

Robert McFadden and Susan Saulny, "DNA in Central Park Jogger Case Spurs Call for New Review," *New York Times*, September 6, 2002.

New York Times, "Houston Seeks Retest of DNA After Audit," March 2, 2003.

———, "Police Identify Top Suspect in Louisiana Serial Killings," May 27, 2003.

Hugh Price, "More Victims in the N.Y. Jogger Case," *San Diego Union Tribune*, December 13, 2002.

William K. Rashbaum, "New York Pursues Old Cases of Rape Based Just on DNA," *New York Times*, August 5, 2003.

San Diego Union Tribune, "Caviar Ring Leaders Receive Sentences," October 29, 2003.

———, "DNA Errors Found in Nine Criminal Cases," May 6, 2003.

———, "DNA Test Frees Man Jailed for Seventeen Years," August 27, 2002.

———, "Exonerated Inmates Toast Their Defenders," September 15, 2002.

———, "House OKs $1 Billion for DNA Testing," November 6, 2003.

———, "Identified Only by DNA, Man Gets Sixty-five Years for Rape," June 27, 2003.

———, "Inmate Free; DNA Clears Him in Three 1985 Rapes," August 26, 2003.

———, "Licked Envelope Nets Arrest in Old Slaying," June 26, 2003.

———, "Slain Cockatoo Stars as Witness in Trial," February, 19, 2003.

David Savage, "'92 Execution Haunts Death Penalty Foes," *Los Angeles Times*, July 22, 2001.

Mindy Sink, "Genetic Pawprints Are Leading Game Wardens to Poachers," *New York Times*, May 26, 1998.

Onell Soto, "Rapist Gets Forty-eight Years in Prison in '93 Case," *San Diego Union Tribune*, October 17, 2002.

Alexander Stille, "New Mission for DNA: Preservation," *New York Times*, February 12, 2000.

Greg Thompson and Emily Williams, "The Thin Blue Line's

New Front Line," *San Diego Union Tribune*, July 27, 2003.

Nicholas Wade, "DNA Changed the World. Now What?" *New York Times*, February 25, 2003.

Victor Weedn and John Hicks, "The Unrealized Potential of DNA Testing," *National Institute of Justice Journal*, December 1997.

John Wilkens, "Convicted of Innocence," *San Diego Union Tribune*, June 15, 2003.

Richard Willing, "White House Seeks to Expand DNA Database to Juveniles," *USA Today*, April 16, 2003.

Michael Wilson, "Exonerated but on Their Own," *New York Times*, May 10, 2003.

Internet Sources

ABC News, "Identical Twins in DNA Dispute," http://abclocal.go.com/wpvi/news/42503-twins.html.

ABCNews.com, "The Future of DNA Evidence," http://abcnews.go.com/sections/us/DailyNews/dnaexpert080499_chat.html.

American Civil Liberties Union, "Alaska to Expand DNA Collection," March 7, 2001. www.aclu.org/news/NewsPrint.cfm?ID=.

———, "DNA Databases Hold More Dangers than Meet the Eye, ACLU Says," March 23, 2000. www.aclu.org/news/NewsPrint.cfm?ID=7886&c=129.

Arctic Science Journeys, "DNA Detectives," www.uaf.edu/seagrant/NewsMedia/98ASJ/04.16.98_DNA.html.

Associated Press, "Spread of Innocence Projects Seen as New Civil Rights Movement," *Dallas Morning News*, June 6, 2002. www.DallasNews.com.

Pam Belluck, "Push in Massachusetts for a Death Penalty," *New York Times*, September 22, 2003. www.nytimes.com.

Eric Berger, "DNA Analysis Becoming More Precise,

Pervasive," *Houston Chronicle*, March 16, 2003. www.Houston Chronicle.com.

British Columbia Institute of Technology, "Poachers Beware: New DNA Forensics Helps Nab Illegal Wildlife Traders," news release, December 19, 2000. www.news releases.bcit.ca/state/forensic-bear.dna.shtml.

CBSNews.com, "DNA Solves Crimes Too," March 29, 2001. www.cbsnews.com/stories/2001/03/29/eveningnews/printable282554.shtml.

———, "Free Testing for Inmates," July 27, 2000. www.cbsnews.com/stories/2000/07/27/national/printable 219466.shtml.

CITES, "Caviar Company, Corporate Officers Sentenced for Illegal Trade, Fraud Scheme; Landmark Fine Assessed," press release, January 21, 2001. www.cites.org/eng/news/cuttings/2001/us-caviar-02-21.shtml.

Rhonda Cook, "DNA Testing Ordered in Case of Man Already Executed," *Atlanta Journal-Constitution*, October 19, 2000. www.truthinjustice.org/felker.htm.

Earthtrust, "Saving Whales with DNA." www.earththrust.org/dnaproj.html.

Rachel Ehrenberg, "High Cost of a Fin," *Mercury News*, February 18, 2003. www.bayarea.com/mid/mercurynews/living/health/5205468.htm?template=contentModules/printstory.jsp.

Environmental News Network, "DNA Technology Busts Wildlife Poachers," CNN.com, May 29, 2000. www.cnn.com/nature.

Kimberly Epler, "Attorneys: DNA Evidence 'Powerful, Compeling,' to Jurors," *North County Times,* www.nctimes.net/news/2002/20020324/609.html.

Georgia Bureau of Investigation, Division of Forensic Sciences, Trace Evidence Section, www.ganet.org/gbi/trace_evidence.html.

Michelle Hibbert, "State and Federal DNA Database Laws Examined," Frontline, www.pbs.org/wgbh/pages/frontline/shows/case/revolution/databases.html.

Innocence Project, "DNA News," www.innocenceproject.org/dnanews/index.php.

Jonathan Kimmelman, "Risking Ethical Insolvency: A Survey of Trends on Criminal DNA Databanking," *Journal of Law, Medicine, Ethics*, Fall 2000. www.aslme.org/pub_jlme/28.3h.php.

Ray Lilley, "Evidence of Illegal Whale Trade Uncovered in New Zealand," Environmental Media Services, May 12, 1998. www.ems.org/whales/endangered_whales_trade.html.

Nicole Litzie, "Whaling: What's Going On at the IWC?" March 11, 1998. http://darwin.bio.uci.edu/sustain/global/sensem/litzil/98.html.

Judy Muller, "Old Crimes Solved with New Technology," ABC News, May 10, 2003. www.abcnews.com.

National DNA Data Bank, "The Birth of DNA Evidence," www.nddb-bndg.org/cases/collin_e.htm.

Online Forum, "Strands of Justice: Do DNA Databanks Infringe on Defendants's Rights?" PBS, www.pbs.org/newshour/forum/july98/dna_databanks05.html.

Michelle Pahl, "U.S. Animal Detectives Fight Crime in Forensics Lab," *National Geographic Today*, April 2, 2003. http://nationalgeographic.com/news/2003.

Frank Phillips, "Science Stressed in Death Penalty," *Boston Globe*, September 24, 2003. www.boston.com

Quantum ABCTV, "Egg Smuggler," March 8, 2001. www.abc.net.au/quantum/S253003htm.

Science and Technology News Network, "DNA Detective," January 25, 2001. www.truthinjustice.org/dna-detective.htm.

The Science Show, "Whale DNA," December 16, 2000. www.abc.net.au/rn/science/ss/stories/s223982.htm.

Vicki Smith, "Forensic Scientist Forms Cold Case Consulting Group," September 5, 2003. www.phillyburbs.com.

David Sommer, "Calzacorto Receives Life Jail Sentence," *Valley Independent*, May 1, 2003. http://livesite.pittsburgh-live.com/x/valleyindependent/news/donora/s_132207.html.

U.S. Department of Justice, introduction to *Handbook of Forensic Services,* www.fbi.gov.

United Press International, "Commentary Faceoff: To Test or Not to Test," ClariNet, September 29, 2003. http://quick start.clarinet/qs_se/webnews/wed/cx/Ufaceoff-dna.Rlul_DST.html.

Joseph Verrengia, "DNA Fingerprinting Identifies Whale Meat in Japan as Endangered," Environmental Media Services, January 28, 1999. www.ems.org/whales/endangered_whales_trade.html.

Wildlife Conservation Society, "Waiter, There's a Shark in My Soup," August, 2003. http://naturalworldtours.co.uk/articles 2003/august/august0203h.htm.

Wired News, "The Debate over DNA Evidence," July 12, 1999. http://wired.com/news/politics/0,128,20670,00.html.

Web Sites

Innocence Project (www.innocenceproject.org). The Innocence Project, based at the Benjamin N. Cardozo School of Law in New York, works to free inmates from prison. Information on cases that have been solved or are pending and how to begin the process of exoneration are available.

Other Media

48 Hours Investigates, "Cry Rape," CBS News, September 20, 2003. Story about solving a twenty-year-old rape case.

National Public Radio, *This American Life*, May 24, 2003. Story about Kathleen Zellner, who worked to free the four boys who confessed to the murder of Lori Roscetti.

Index

Picture Credits

Cover Image: AP/Wide World Photos

AP/Wide World Photos, 29, 31, 33, 36, 37, 38, 45, 46, 48, 71, 72, 75, 77, 78, 81, 84

© A. Barrington Brown/Photo Researchers, Inc., 11

© Vince Bucci/Reuters/Landov, 7

© Frank H. Colon-Pool/Getty Images, 41

© ENGLISH GREG/CORBIS SYGMA, 24

© EPA/Landov, 59

© EPA/Kei Ishida/Landov, 66

© EPA/Paul Hilton/Landov, 65

© Stephen Ferry/Liaison/Getty Images, 55, 56

© Patrick Harbron/Landov, 47

Robin Hunter/U.S. Fish and Wildlife Service, 67

© James King-Holmes/ICRF/Photo Researchers, Inc., 18

PhotoDisc, 62

© Frank Polich/Reuters/Landov, 53

© Denis Poroy/Reuters/Landov, 8

© Roger Ressmeyer/CORBIS, 21

© Reuters NewMedia Inc./CORBIS, 30

© Terry Smith/Time Life Pictures/Getty Images, 17

About the Author

Tina Kafka worked as a freelance writer and editor after graduating from the University of California at San Diego, but put the pen aside for ten years to become an elementary schoolteacher. She currently teaches science at Explorer Elementary Charter School in La Jolla, California, where she is also the curriculum coordinator. She also wrote *Making Equipment for Outdoor Adventures*, which will soon be published by Dorling-Kindersley.

Kafka has three creative children. She and her husband Zoltan, who is also a teacher, spend their summers fixing up their craftsman-style house, camping, and traveling to places they have never been with their hand-built teardrop trailer.